The Law School Admission Council (LSAC) is a nonprofit corporation that provides unique, state-of-the-art admission products and services to ease the admission process for law schools and their applicants worldwide. Currently, 218 law schools in the United States, Canada, and Australia are members of the Council and benefit from LSAC's services.

LSAC fees, policies, and procedures relating to, but not limited to, test registration, test administration, test score reporting, misconduct and irregularities, Credential Assembly Service (CAS), and other matters may change without notice at any time. Up-to-date LSAC policies and procedures are available at LSAC.org.

ISBN-13: 978-0-9860455-0-9

Print number
10 9 8 7 6 5 4 3 2 1

TABLE OF CONTENTS

• Introduction to the LSAT 1

  • Scoring 1
    • Test Score Accuracy—Reliability and Standard Error of Measurement............................1
    • Adjustments for Variation in Test Difficulty 1
    • Research on the LSAT 1
    • To Inquire About Test Questions 2

  • How This PrepTest Differs From an Actual LSAT 2

  • The Three LSAT Multiple-Choice Question Types..2
    • Analytical Reasoning Questions 2
    • Logical Reasoning Questions...3
    • Reading Comprehension Questions 4

  • The Writing Sample..5

  • Taking the PrepTest Under Simulated LSAT Conditions 6

• Answer Sheet 7

• The PrepTest 9

• LSAT Writing Sample Topic...43

• Writing Sample Response Sheet..45

• Computing Your Score 47

• Answer Key..48

INTRODUCTION TO THE LSAT

The Law School Admission Test is a half-day standardized test required for admission to all ABA-approved law schools, most Canadian law schools, and many other law schools. It consists of five 35-minute sections of multiple-choice questions. Four of the five sections contribute to the test taker's score. These sections include one Reading Comprehension section, one Analytical Reasoning section, and two Logical Reasoning sections. The unscored section, commonly referred to as the variable section, typically is used to pretest new test questions or to preequate new test forms. The placement of this section in the LSAT will vary. A 35-minute writing sample is administered at the end of the test. The writing sample is not scored by LSAC, but copies are sent to all law schools to which you apply. The score scale for the LSAT is 120 to 180.

The LSAT is designed to measure skills considered essential for success in law school: the reading and comprehension of complex texts with accuracy and insight; the organization and management of information and the ability to draw reasonable inferences from it; the ability to think critically; and the analysis and evaluation of the reasoning and arguments of others.

The LSAT provides a standard measure of acquired reading and verbal reasoning skills that law schools can use as one of several factors in assessing applicants.

For up-to-date information about LSAC's services, go to our website, LSAC.org.

SCORING

Your LSAT score is based on the number of questions you answer correctly (the raw score). There is no deduction for incorrect answers, and all questions count equally. In other words, there is no penalty for guessing.

Test Score Accuracy—Reliability and Standard Error of Measurement

Candidates perform at different levels on different occasions for reasons quite unrelated to the characteristics of a test itself. The accuracy of test scores is best described by the use of two related statistical terms: reliability and standard error of measurement.

Reliability is a measure of how consistently a test measures the skills being assessed. The higher the reliability coefficient for a test, the more certain we can be that test takers would get very similar scores if they took the test again.

LSAC reports an internal consistency measure of reliability for every test form. Reliability can vary from 0.00 to 1.00, and a test with no measurement error would have a reliability coefficient of 1.00 (never attained in practice). Reliability coefficients for past LSAT forms have ranged from .90 to .95, indicating a high degree of consistency for these tests. LSAC expects the reliability of the LSAT to continue to fall within the same range.

LSAC also reports the amount of measurement error associated with each test form, a concept known as the standard error of measurement (SEM). The SEM, which is usually about 2.6 points, indicates how close a test taker's observed score is likely to be to his or her true score. True scores are theoretical scores that would be obtained from perfectly reliable tests with no measurement error—scores never known in practice.

Score bands, or ranges of scores that contain a test taker's true score a certain percentage of the time, can be derived using the SEM. LSAT score bands are constructed by adding and subtracting the (rounded) SEM to and from an actual LSAT score (e.g., the LSAT score, plus or minus 3 points). Scores near 120 or 180 have asymmetrical bands. Score bands constructed in this manner will contain an individual's true score approximately 68 percent of the time.

Measurement error also must be taken into account when comparing LSAT scores of two test takers. It is likely that small differences in scores are due to measurement error rather than to meaningful differences in ability. The standard error of score differences provides some guidance as to the importance of differences between two scores. The standard error of score differences is approximately 1.4 times larger than the standard error of measurement for the individual scores.

Thus, a test score should be regarded as a useful but approximate measure of a test taker's abilities as measured by the test, not as an exact determination of his or her abilities. LSAC encourages law schools to examine the range of scores within the interval that probably contains the test taker's true score (e.g., the test taker's score band) rather than solely interpret the reported score alone.

Adjustments for Variation in Test Difficulty

All test forms of the LSAT reported on the same score scale are designed to measure the same abilities, but one test form may be slightly easier or more difficult than another. The scores from different test forms are made comparable through a statistical procedure known as equating. As a result of equating, a given scaled score earned on different test forms reflects the same level of ability.

Research on the LSAT

Summaries of LSAT validity studies and other LSAT research can be found in member law school libraries and at LSAC.org.

To Inquire About Test Questions

If you find what you believe to be an error or ambiguity in a test question that affects your response to the question, contact LSAC by e-mail: LSATTS@LSAC.org, or write to Law School Admission Council, Test Development Group, PO Box 40, Newtown, PA 18940-0040.

HOW THIS PREPTEST DIFFERS FROM AN ACTUAL LSAT

This PrepTest is made up of the scored sections and writing sample from the actual disclosed LSAT administered in December 2013. However, it does not contain the extra, variable section that is used to pretest new test items of one of the three multiple-choice question types. The three multiple-choice question types may be in a different order in an actual LSAT than in this PrepTest. This is because the order of these question types is intentionally varied for each administration of the test.

THE THREE LSAT MULTIPLE-CHOICE QUESTION TYPES

The multiple-choice questions that make up most of the LSAT reflect a broad range of academic disciplines and are intended to give no advantage to candidates from a particular academic background.

The five sections of the test contain three different question types. The following material presents a general discussion of the nature of each question type and some strategies that can be used in answering them.

Analytical Reasoning Questions

Analytical Reasoning questions are designed to assess the ability to consider a group of facts and rules, and, given those facts and rules, determine what could or must be true. The specific scenarios associated with these questions are usually unrelated to law, since they are intended to be accessible to a wide range of test takers. However, the skills tested parallel those involved in determining what could or must be the case given a set of regulations, the terms of a contract, or the facts of a legal case in relation to the law. In Analytical Reasoning questions, you are asked to reason deductively from a set of statements and rules or principles that describe relationships among persons, things, or events.

Analytical Reasoning questions appear in sets, with each set based on a single passage. The passage used for each set of questions describes common ordering relationships or grouping relationships, or a combination of both types of relationships. Examples include scheduling employees for work shifts, assigning instructors to class sections,

ordering tasks according to priority, and distributing grants for projects.

Analytical Reasoning questions test a range of deductive reasoning skills. These include:

- Comprehending the basic structure of a set of relationships by determining a complete solution to the problem posed (for example, an acceptable seating arrangement of all six diplomats around a table)

- Reasoning with conditional ("if-then") statements and recognizing logically equivalent formulations of such statements

- Inferring what could be true or must be true from given facts and rules

- Inferring what could be true or must be true from given facts and rules together with new information in the form of an additional or substitute fact or rule

- Recognizing when two statements are logically equivalent in context by identifying a condition or rule that could replace one of the original conditions while still resulting in the same possible outcomes

Analytical Reasoning questions reflect the kinds of detailed analyses of relationships and sets of constraints that a law student must perform in legal problem solving. For example, an Analytical Reasoning passage might describe six diplomats being seated around a table, following certain rules of protocol as to who can sit where. You, the test taker, must answer questions about the logical implications of given and new information. For example, you may be asked who can sit between diplomats X and Y, or who cannot sit next to X if W sits next to Y. Similarly, if you were a student in law school, you might be asked to analyze a scenario involving a set of particular circumstances and a set of governing rules in the form of constitutional provisions, statutes, administrative codes, or prior rulings that have been upheld. You might then be asked to determine the legal options in the scenario: what is required given the scenario, what is permissible given the scenario, and what is prohibited given the scenario. Or you might be asked to develop a "theory" for the case: when faced with an incomplete set of facts about the case, you must fill in the picture based on what is implied by the facts that are known. The problem could be elaborated by the addition of new information or hypotheticals.

No formal training in logic is required to answer these questions correctly. Analytical Reasoning questions are intended to be answered using knowledge, skills, and reasoning ability generally expected of college students and graduates.

Suggested Approach

Some people may prefer to answer first those questions about a passage that seem less difficult and then those that seem more difficult. In general, it is best to finish one passage before starting on another, because much time can be lost in returning to a passage and reestablishing familiarity with its relationships. However, if you are having great difficulty on one particular set of questions and are spending too much time on them, it may be to your advantage to skip that set of questions and go on to the next passage, returning to the problematic set of questions after you have finished the other questions in the section.

Do not assume that because the conditions for a set of questions look long or complicated, the questions based on those conditions will be especially difficult.

Read the passage carefully. Careful reading and analysis are necessary to determine the exact nature of the relationships involved in an Analytical Reasoning passage. Some relationships are fixed (for example, P and R must always work on the same project). Other relationships are variable (for example, Q must be assigned to either team 1 or team 3). Some relationships that are not stated explicitly in the conditions are implied by and can be deduced from those that are stated (for example, if one condition about paintings in a display specifies that Painting K must be to the left of Painting Y, and another specifies that Painting W must be to the left of Painting K, then it can be deduced that Painting W must be to the left of Painting Y).

In reading the conditions, do not introduce unwarranted assumptions. For instance, in a set of questions establishing relationships of height and weight among the members of a team, do not assume that a person who is taller than another person must weigh more than that person. As another example, suppose a set involves ordering and a question in the set asks what must be true if both X and Y must be earlier than Z; in this case, do not assume that X must be earlier than Y merely because X is mentioned before Y. All the information needed to answer each question is provided in the passage and the question itself.

The conditions are designed to be as clear as possible. Do not interpret the conditions as if they were intended to trick you. For example, if a question asks how many people could be eligible to serve on a committee, consider only those people named in the passage unless directed otherwise. When in doubt, read the conditions in their most obvious sense. Remember, however, that the language in the conditions is intended to be read for precise meaning. It is essential to pay particular attention to words that describe or limit relationships, such as "only," "exactly," "never," "always," "must be," "cannot be," and the like.

The result of this careful reading will be a clear picture of the structure of the relationships involved, including the kinds of relationships permitted, the participants in the relationships, and the range of possible actions or attributes for these participants.

Keep in mind question independence. Each question should be considered separately from the other questions in its set. No information, except what is given in the original conditions, should be carried over from one question to another.

In some cases a question will simply ask for conclusions to be drawn from the conditions as originally given. Some questions may, however, add information to the original conditions or temporarily suspend or replace one of the original conditions for the purpose of that question only. For example, if Question 1 adds the supposition "if P is sitting at table 2 ...," this supposition should NOT be carried over to any other question in the set.

Consider highlighting text and using diagrams. Many people find it useful to underline key points in the passage and in each question. In addition, it may prove very helpful to draw a diagram to assist you in finding the solution to the problem.

In preparing for the test, you may wish to experiment with different types of diagrams. For a scheduling problem, a simple calendar-like diagram may be helpful. For a grouping problem, an array of labeled columns or rows may be useful.

Even though most people find diagrams to be very helpful, some people seldom use them, and for some individual questions no one will need a diagram. There is by no means universal agreement on which kind of diagram is best for which problem or in which cases a diagram is most useful. Do not be concerned if a particular problem in the test seems to be best approached without the use of a diagram.

Logical Reasoning Questions

Arguments are a fundamental part of the law, and analyzing arguments is a key element of legal analysis. Training in the law builds on a foundation of basic reasoning skills. Law students must draw on the skills of analyzing, evaluating, constructing, and refuting arguments. They need to be able to identify what information is relevant to an issue or argument and what impact further evidence might have. They need to be able to reconcile opposing positions and use arguments to persuade others.

Logical Reasoning questions evaluate the ability to analyze, critically evaluate, and complete arguments as they occur in ordinary language. The questions are based on short arguments drawn from a wide variety of sources, including newspapers, general interest magazines, scholarly publications, advertisements, and informal discourse. These arguments mirror legal reasoning in the types of arguments presented and in their complexity, though few of the arguments actually have law as a subject matter.

Each Logical Reasoning question requires you to read and comprehend a short passage, then answer one question (or, rarely, two questions) about it. The questions are designed to assess a wide range of skills involved in thinking critically, with an emphasis on skills that are central to legal reasoning.

These skills include:

- Recognizing the parts of an argument and their relationships

- Recognizing similarities and differences between patterns of reasoning

- Drawing well-supported conclusions

- Reasoning by analogy

- Recognizing misunderstandings or points of disagreement

- Determining how additional evidence affects an argument

- Detecting assumptions made by particular arguments

- Identifying and applying principles or rules

- Identifying flaws in arguments

- Identifying explanations

The questions do not presuppose specialized knowledge of logical terminology. For example, you will not be expected to know the meaning of specialized terms such as "ad hominem" or "syllogism." On the other hand, you will be expected to understand and critique the reasoning contained in arguments. This requires that you possess a university-level understanding of widely used concepts such as argument, premise, assumption, and conclusion.

Suggested Approach

Read each question carefully. Make sure that you understand the meaning of each part of the question. Make sure that you understand the meaning of each answer choice and the ways in which it may or may not relate to the question posed.

Do not pick a response simply because it is a true statement. Although true, it may not answer the question posed.

Answer each question on the basis of the information that is given, even if you do not agree with it. Work within the context provided by the passage. LSAT questions do not involve any tricks or hidden meanings.

Reading Comprehension Questions

Both law school and the practice of law revolve around extensive reading of highly varied, dense, argumentative, and expository texts (for example, cases, codes, contracts, briefs, decisions, evidence). This reading must be exacting, distinguishing precisely what is said from what is not said. It involves comparison, analysis, synthesis, and application (for example, of principles and rules). It involves drawing appropriate inferences and applying ideas and arguments to new contexts. Law school reading also requires the ability to grasp unfamiliar subject matter and the ability to penetrate difficult and challenging material.

The purpose of LSAT Reading Comprehension questions is to measure the ability to read, with understanding and insight, examples of lengthy and complex materials similar to those commonly encountered in law school. The Reading Comprehension section of the LSAT contains four sets of reading questions, each set consisting of a selection of reading material followed by five to eight questions. The reading selection in three of the four sets consists of a single reading passage; the other set contains two related shorter passages. Sets with two passages are a variant of Reading Comprehension called Comparative Reading, which was introduced in June 2007.

Comparative Reading questions concern the relationships between the two passages, such as those of generalization/instance, principle/application, or point/counterpoint. Law school work often requires reading two or more texts in conjunction with each other and understanding their relationships. For example, a law student may read a trial court decision together with an appellate court decision that overturns it, or identify the fact pattern from a hypothetical suit together with the potentially controlling case law.

Reading selections for LSAT Reading Comprehension questions are drawn from a wide range of subjects in the humanities, the social sciences, the biological and physical sciences, and areas related to the law. Generally, the selections are densely written, use high-level vocabulary, and contain sophisticated argument or complex rhetorical structure (for example, multiple points of view). Reading Comprehension questions require you to read carefully and accurately, to determine the relationships among the various parts of the reading selection, and to draw reasonable inferences from the material in the selection. The questions may ask about the following characteristics of a passage or pair of passages:

- The main idea or primary purpose

- Information that is explicitly stated

- Information or ideas that can be inferred

- The meaning or purpose of words or phrases as used in context

- The organization or structure

- The application of information in the selection to a new context

- Principles that function in the selection

- Analogies to claims or arguments in the selection

- An author's attitude as revealed in the tone of a passage or the language used

- The impact of new information on claims or arguments in the selection

Suggested Approach

Since reading selections are drawn from many different disciplines and sources, you should not be discouraged if you encounter material with which you are not familiar. It is important to remember that questions are to be answered exclusively on the basis of the information provided in the selection. There is no particular knowledge that you are expected to bring to the test, and you should not make inferences based on any prior knowledge of a subject that you may have. You may, however, wish to defer working on a set of questions that seems particularly difficult or unfamiliar until after you have dealt with sets you find easier.

Strategies. One question that often arises in connection with Reading Comprehension has to do with the most effective and efficient order in which to read the selections and questions. Possible approaches include:

- reading the selection very closely and then answering the questions;

- reading the questions first, reading the selection closely, and then returning to the questions; or

- skimming the selection and questions very quickly, then rereading the selection closely and answering the questions.

Test takers are different, and the best strategy for one might not be the best strategy for another. In preparing for the test, therefore, you might want to experiment with the different strategies and decide what works most effectively for you.

Remember that your strategy must be effective under timed conditions. For this reason, the first strategy—reading the selection very closely and then answering the questions—may be the most effective for you. Nonetheless, if you believe that one of the other strategies

might be more effective for you, you should try it out and assess your performance using it.

Reading the selection. Whatever strategy you choose, you should give the passage or pair of passages at least one careful reading before answering the questions. Try to distinguish main ideas from supporting ideas, and opinions or attitudes from factual, objective information. Note transitions from one idea to the next and identify the relationships among the different ideas or parts of a passage, or between the two passages in Comparative Reading sets. Consider how and why an author makes points and draws conclusions. Be sensitive to implications of what the passages say.

You may find it helpful to mark key parts of passages. For example, you might underline main ideas or important arguments, and you might circle transitional words— "although," "nevertheless," "correspondingly," and the like—that will help you map the structure of a passage. Also, you might note descriptive words that will help you identify an author's attitude toward a particular idea or person.

Answering the Questions

- Always read all the answer choices before selecting the best answer. The best answer choice is the one that most accurately and completely answers the question being posed.

- Respond to the specific question being asked. Do not pick an answer choice simply because it is a true statement. For example, picking a true statement might yield an incorrect answer to a question in which you are asked to identify an author's position on an issue, since you are not being asked to evaluate the truth of the author's position but only to correctly identify what that position is.

- Answer the questions only on the basis of the information provided in the selection. Your own views, interpretations, or opinions, and those you have heard from others, may sometimes conflict with those expressed in a reading selection; however, you are expected to work within the context provided by the reading selection. You should not expect to agree with everything you encounter in Reading Comprehension passages.

THE WRITING SAMPLE

On the day of the test, you will be asked to write one sample essay. LSAC does not score the writing sample, but copies are sent to all law schools to which you apply. According to a 2006 LSAC survey of 157 United States and Canadian law schools, almost all use the writing sample in evaluating at least some applications for admission. Failure to respond to writing sample prompts and frivolous responses have been used by law schools as grounds for rejection of applications for admission.

In developing and implementing the writing sample portion of the LSAT, LSAC has operated on the following premises: First, law schools and the legal profession value highly the ability to communicate effectively in writing. Second, it is important to encourage potential law students to develop effective writing skills. Third, a sample of an applicant's writing, produced under controlled conditions, is a potentially useful indication of that person's writing ability. Fourth, the writing sample can serve as an independent check on other writing submitted by applicants as part of the admission process. Finally, writing samples may be useful for diagnostic purposes related to improving a candidate's writing.

The writing prompt presents a decision problem. You are asked to make a choice between two positions or courses of action. Both of the choices are defensible, and you are given criteria and facts on which to base your decision. There is no "right" or "wrong" position to take on the topic, so the quality of each test taker's response is a function not of which choice is made, but of how well or poorly the choice is supported and how well or poorly the other choice is criticized.

The LSAT writing prompt was designed and validated by legal education professionals. Since it involves writing based on fact sets and criteria, the writing sample gives applicants the opportunity to demonstrate the type of argumentative writing that is required in law school, although the topics are usually nonlegal.

You will have 35 minutes in which to plan and write an essay on the topic you receive. Read the topic and the accompanying directions carefully. You will probably find it best to spend a few minutes considering the topic and organizing your thoughts before you begin writing. In your essay, be sure to develop your ideas fully, leaving time, if possible, to review what you have written. Do not write on a topic other than the one specified. Writing on a topic of your own choice is not acceptable.

No special knowledge is required or expected for this writing exercise. Law schools are interested in the reasoning, clarity, organization, language usage, and writing mechanics displayed in your essay. How well you write is more important than how much you write. Confine your essay to the blocked, lined area on the front and back of the separate Writing Sample Response Sheet. Only that area will be reproduced for law schools. Be sure that your writing is legible.

TAKING THE PREPTEST UNDER SIMULATED LSAT CONDITIONS

One important way to prepare for the LSAT is to simulate the day of the test by taking a practice test under actual

time constraints. Taking a practice test under timed conditions helps you to estimate the amount of time you can afford to spend on each question in a section and to determine the question types on which you may need additional practice.

Since the LSAT is a timed test, it is important to use your allotted time wisely. During the test, you may work only on the section designated by the test supervisor. You cannot devote extra time to a difficult section and make up that time on a section you find easier. In pacing yourself, and checking your answers, you should think of each section of the test as a separate minitest.

Be sure that you answer every question on the test. When you do not know the correct answer to a question, first eliminate the responses that you know are incorrect, then make your best guess among the remaining choices. Do not be afraid to guess as there is no penalty for incorrect answers.

When you take a practice test, abide by all the requirements specified in the directions and keep strictly within the specified time limits. Work without a rest period. When you take an actual test, you will have only a short break—usually 10–15 minutes—after SECTION III.

When taken under conditions as much like actual testing conditions as possible, a practice test provides very useful preparation for taking the LSAT.

Official directions for the four multiple-choice sections and the writing sample are included in this PrepTest so that you can approximate actual testing conditions as you practice.

To take the test:

- Set a timer for 35 minutes. Answer all the questions in SECTION I of this PrepTest. Stop working on that section when the 35 minutes have elapsed.

- Repeat, allowing yourself 35 minutes each for sections II, III, and IV.

- Set the timer again for 35 minutes, then prepare your response to the writing sample topic at the end of this PrepTest.

- Refer to "Computing Your Score" for the PrepTest for instruction on evaluating your performance. An answer key is provided for that purpose.

The practice test that follows consists of four sections corresponding to the four scored sections of the December 2013 LSAT. Also reprinted is the December 2013 unscored writing sample topic.

General Directions for the LSAT Answer Sheet

The actual testing time for this portion of the test will be 2 hours 55 minutes. There are five sections, each with a time limit of 35 minutes. The supervisor will tell you when to begin and end each section. If you finish a section before time is called, you may check your work on that section **only**; do not turn to any other section of the test book and do not work on any other section either in the test book or on the answer sheet.

There are several different types of questions on the test, and each question type has its own directions. **Be sure you understand the directions for each question type before attempting to answer any questions in that section.**

Not everyone will finish all the questions in the time allowed. Do not hurry, but work steadily and as quickly as you can without sacrificing accuracy. You are advised to use your time effectively. If a question seems too difficult, go on to the next one and return to the difficult question after completing the section. **MARK THE BEST ANSWER YOU CAN FOR EVERY QUESTION. NO DEDUCTIONS WILL BE MADE FOR WRONG ANSWERS. YOUR SCORE WILL BE BASED ONLY ON THE NUMBER OF QUESTIONS YOU ANSWER CORRECTLY.**

ALL YOUR ANSWERS MUST BE MARKED ON THE ANSWER SHEET. Answer spaces for each question are lettered to correspond with the letters of the potential answers to each question in the test book. After you have decided which of the answers is correct, blacken the corresponding space on the answer sheet. **BE SURE THAT EACH MARK IS BLACK AND COMPLETELY FILLS THE ANSWER SPACE.** Give only one answer to each question. If you change an answer, be sure that all previous marks are **erased completely.** Since the answer sheet is machine scored, incomplete erasures may be interpreted as intended answers. **ANSWERS RECORDED IN THE TEST BOOK WILL NOT BE SCORED.**

There may be more question numbers on this answer sheet than there are questions in a section. Do not be concerned, but be certain that the section and number of the question you are answering matches the answer sheet section and question number. Additional answer spaces in any answer sheet section should be left blank. Begin your next section in the number one answer space for that section.

LSAC takes various steps to ensure that answer sheets are returned from test centers in a timely manner for processing. In the unlikely event that an answer sheet is not received, LSAC will permit the examinee either to retest at no additional fee or to receive a refund of his or her LSAT fee. **THESE REMEDIES ARE THE ONLY REMEDIES AVAILABLE IN THE UNLIKELY EVENT THAT AN ANSWER SHEET IS NOT RECEIVED BY LSAC.**

Score Cancellation

Complete this section only if you are absolutely certain you want to cancel your score. **A CANCELLATION REQUEST CANNOT BE RESCINDED. IF YOU ARE AT ALL UNCERTAIN, YOU SHOULD NOT COMPLETE THIS SECTION.**

To cancel your score from this administration, you **must:**

A. fill in both ovals here ...... ○ ○
        AND
B. read the following statement. Then sign your name and enter the date.
YOUR SIGNATURE ALONE IS NOT SUFFICIENT FOR SCORE CANCELLATION. BOTH OVALS ABOVE MUST BE FILLED IN FOR SCANNING EQUIPMENT TO RECOGNIZE YOUR REQUEST FOR SCORE CANCELLATION.

I certify that I wish to cancel my test score from this administration. I understand that my request is irreversible and that my score will not be sent to me or to the law schools to which I apply.

Sign your name in full
_____

Date
_____

FOR LSAC USE ONLY ⬭

HOW DID YOU PREPARE FOR THE LSAT?
(Select all that apply.)

Responses to this item are voluntary and will be used for statistical research purposes only.

○ By studying the free sample questions available on LSAC's website.
○ By taking the free sample LSAT available on LSAC's website.
○ By working through official LSAT *PrepTests*, *ItemWise*, and/or other LSAC test prep products.
○ By using LSAT prep books or software **not** published by LSAC.
○ By attending a commercial test preparation or coaching course.
○ By attending a test preparation or coaching course offered through an undergraduate institution.
○ Self study.
○ Other preparation.
○ No preparation.

CERTIFYING STATEMENT

Please write the following statement. Sign and date.

I certify that I am the examinee whose name appears on this answer sheet and that I am here to take the LSAT for the sole purpose of being considered for admission to law school. I further certify that I will neither assist nor receive assistance from any other candidate, and I agree not to copy, retain, or transmit examination questions in any form or discuss them with any other person.

_____
_____
_____
_____
_____
_____
_____
_____
_____

SIGNATURE: _____ TODAY'S DATE: ___/___/___
                                            MONTH DAY YEAR

INSTRUCTIONS FOR COMPLETING THE BIOGRAPHICAL AREA ARE ON THE BACK COVER OF YOUR TEST BOOKLET.
USE ONLY A NO. 2 OR HB PENCIL TO COMPLETE THIS ANSWER SHEET. DO NOT USE INK.

A

1 LAST NAME | **FIRST NAME** | **MI**

2 LAST 4 DIGITS OF SOCIAL SECURITY/ SOCIAL INSURANCE NO.

L

3 LSAC ACCOUNT NUMBER

4 CENTER NUMBER

5 DATE OF BIRTH

MONTH	DAY	YEAR
○ Jan		
○ Feb		
○ Mar		
○ Apr		
○ May		
○ June		
○ July		
○ Aug		
○ Sept		
○ Oct		
○ Nov		
○ Dec		

6 TEST FORM CODE

7 RACIAL/ETHNIC DESCRIPTION
Mark one or more

○ 1 Amer. Indian/Alaska Na
○ 2 Asian
○ 3 Black/African America
○ 4 Canadian Aboriginal
○ 5 Caucasian/White
○ 6 Hispanic/Latino
○ 7 Native Hawaiian/ Other Pacific Islander
○ 8 Puerto Rican
○ 9 TSI/Aboriginal Austra

8 GENDER
○ Male
○ Female

9 DOMINANT LANGUAGE
○ English
○ Other

10 ENGLISH FLUENCY
○ Yes
○ No

11 TEST DATE
/ /
MONTH DAY YEAR

12 TEST FORM

13 TEST BOOK SERIAL NO.

═══ **Law School Admission Test** ═══

Mark one and only one answer to each question. Be sure to fill in completely the space for your intended answer choice. If you erase, do so completely. Make no stray marks.

SECTION 1	SECTION 2	SECTION 3	SECTION 4	SECTION 5
1 Ⓐ Ⓑ Ⓒ Ⓓ Ⓔ	1 Ⓐ Ⓑ Ⓒ Ⓓ Ⓔ	1 Ⓐ Ⓑ Ⓒ Ⓓ Ⓔ	1 Ⓐ Ⓑ Ⓒ Ⓓ Ⓔ	1 Ⓐ Ⓑ Ⓒ Ⓓ Ⓔ
2 Ⓐ Ⓑ Ⓒ Ⓓ Ⓔ	2 Ⓐ Ⓑ Ⓒ Ⓓ Ⓔ	2 Ⓐ Ⓑ Ⓒ Ⓓ Ⓔ	2 Ⓐ Ⓑ Ⓒ Ⓓ Ⓔ	2 Ⓐ Ⓑ Ⓒ Ⓓ Ⓔ
3 Ⓐ Ⓑ Ⓒ Ⓓ Ⓔ	3 Ⓐ Ⓑ Ⓒ Ⓓ Ⓔ	3 Ⓐ Ⓑ Ⓒ Ⓓ Ⓔ	3 Ⓐ Ⓑ Ⓒ Ⓓ Ⓔ	3 Ⓐ Ⓑ Ⓒ Ⓓ Ⓔ
4 Ⓐ Ⓑ Ⓒ Ⓓ Ⓔ	4 Ⓐ Ⓑ Ⓒ Ⓓ Ⓔ	4 Ⓐ Ⓑ Ⓒ Ⓓ Ⓔ	4 Ⓐ Ⓑ Ⓒ Ⓓ Ⓔ	4 Ⓐ Ⓑ Ⓒ Ⓓ Ⓔ
5 Ⓐ Ⓑ Ⓒ Ⓓ Ⓔ	5 Ⓐ Ⓑ Ⓒ Ⓓ Ⓔ	5 Ⓐ Ⓑ Ⓒ Ⓓ Ⓔ	5 Ⓐ Ⓑ Ⓒ Ⓓ Ⓔ	5 Ⓐ Ⓑ Ⓒ Ⓓ Ⓔ
6 Ⓐ Ⓑ Ⓒ Ⓓ Ⓔ	6 Ⓐ Ⓑ Ⓒ Ⓓ Ⓔ	6 Ⓐ Ⓑ Ⓒ Ⓓ Ⓔ	6 Ⓐ Ⓑ Ⓒ Ⓓ Ⓔ	6 Ⓐ Ⓑ Ⓒ Ⓓ Ⓔ
7 Ⓐ Ⓑ Ⓒ Ⓓ Ⓔ	7 Ⓐ Ⓑ Ⓒ Ⓓ Ⓔ	7 Ⓐ Ⓑ Ⓒ Ⓓ Ⓔ	7 Ⓐ Ⓑ Ⓒ Ⓓ Ⓔ	7 Ⓐ Ⓑ Ⓒ Ⓓ Ⓔ
8 Ⓐ Ⓑ Ⓒ Ⓓ Ⓔ	8 Ⓐ Ⓑ Ⓒ Ⓓ Ⓔ	8 Ⓐ Ⓑ Ⓒ Ⓓ Ⓔ	8 Ⓐ Ⓑ Ⓒ Ⓓ Ⓔ	8 Ⓐ Ⓑ Ⓒ Ⓓ Ⓔ
9 Ⓐ Ⓑ Ⓒ Ⓓ Ⓔ	9 Ⓐ Ⓑ Ⓒ Ⓓ Ⓔ	9 Ⓐ Ⓑ Ⓒ Ⓓ Ⓔ	9 Ⓐ Ⓑ Ⓒ Ⓓ Ⓔ	9 Ⓐ Ⓑ Ⓒ Ⓓ Ⓔ
10 Ⓐ Ⓑ Ⓒ Ⓓ Ⓔ	10 Ⓐ Ⓑ Ⓒ Ⓓ Ⓔ	10 Ⓐ Ⓑ Ⓒ Ⓓ Ⓔ	10 Ⓐ Ⓑ Ⓒ Ⓓ Ⓔ	10 Ⓐ Ⓑ Ⓒ Ⓓ Ⓔ
11 Ⓐ Ⓑ Ⓒ Ⓓ Ⓔ	11 Ⓐ Ⓑ Ⓒ Ⓓ Ⓔ	11 Ⓐ Ⓑ Ⓒ Ⓓ Ⓔ	11 Ⓐ Ⓑ Ⓒ Ⓓ Ⓔ	11 Ⓐ Ⓑ Ⓒ Ⓓ Ⓔ
12 Ⓐ Ⓑ Ⓒ Ⓓ Ⓔ	12 Ⓐ Ⓑ Ⓒ Ⓓ Ⓔ	12 Ⓐ Ⓑ Ⓒ Ⓓ Ⓔ	12 Ⓐ Ⓑ Ⓒ Ⓓ Ⓔ	12 Ⓐ Ⓑ Ⓒ Ⓓ Ⓔ
13 Ⓐ Ⓑ Ⓒ Ⓓ Ⓔ	13 Ⓐ Ⓑ Ⓒ Ⓓ Ⓔ	13 Ⓐ Ⓑ Ⓒ Ⓓ Ⓔ	13 Ⓐ Ⓑ Ⓒ Ⓓ Ⓔ	13 Ⓐ Ⓑ Ⓒ Ⓓ Ⓔ
14 Ⓐ Ⓑ Ⓒ Ⓓ Ⓔ	14 Ⓐ Ⓑ Ⓒ Ⓓ Ⓔ	14 Ⓐ Ⓑ Ⓒ Ⓓ Ⓔ	14 Ⓐ Ⓑ Ⓒ Ⓓ Ⓔ	14 Ⓐ Ⓑ Ⓒ Ⓓ Ⓔ
15 Ⓐ Ⓑ Ⓒ Ⓓ Ⓔ	15 Ⓐ Ⓑ Ⓒ Ⓓ Ⓔ	15 Ⓐ Ⓑ Ⓒ Ⓓ Ⓔ	15 Ⓐ Ⓑ Ⓒ Ⓓ Ⓔ	15 Ⓐ Ⓑ Ⓒ Ⓓ Ⓔ
16 Ⓐ Ⓑ Ⓒ Ⓓ Ⓔ	16 Ⓐ Ⓑ Ⓒ Ⓓ Ⓔ	16 Ⓐ Ⓑ Ⓒ Ⓓ Ⓔ	16 Ⓐ Ⓑ Ⓒ Ⓓ Ⓔ	16 Ⓐ Ⓑ Ⓒ Ⓓ Ⓔ
17 Ⓐ Ⓑ Ⓒ Ⓓ Ⓔ	17 Ⓐ Ⓑ Ⓒ Ⓓ Ⓔ	17 Ⓐ Ⓑ Ⓒ Ⓓ Ⓔ	17 Ⓐ Ⓑ Ⓒ Ⓓ Ⓔ	17 Ⓐ Ⓑ Ⓒ Ⓓ Ⓔ
18 Ⓐ Ⓑ Ⓒ Ⓓ Ⓔ	18 Ⓐ Ⓑ Ⓒ Ⓓ Ⓔ	18 Ⓐ Ⓑ Ⓒ Ⓓ Ⓔ	18 Ⓐ Ⓑ Ⓒ Ⓓ Ⓔ	18 Ⓐ Ⓑ Ⓒ Ⓓ Ⓔ
19 Ⓐ Ⓑ Ⓒ Ⓓ Ⓔ	19 Ⓐ Ⓑ Ⓒ Ⓓ Ⓔ	19 Ⓐ Ⓑ Ⓒ Ⓓ Ⓔ	19 Ⓐ Ⓑ Ⓒ Ⓓ Ⓔ	19 Ⓐ Ⓑ Ⓒ Ⓓ Ⓔ
20 Ⓐ Ⓑ Ⓒ Ⓓ Ⓔ	20 Ⓐ Ⓑ Ⓒ Ⓓ Ⓔ	20 Ⓐ Ⓑ Ⓒ Ⓓ Ⓔ	20 Ⓐ Ⓑ Ⓒ Ⓓ Ⓔ	20 Ⓐ Ⓑ Ⓒ Ⓓ Ⓔ
21 Ⓐ Ⓑ Ⓒ Ⓓ Ⓔ	21 Ⓐ Ⓑ Ⓒ Ⓓ Ⓔ	21 Ⓐ Ⓑ Ⓒ Ⓓ Ⓔ	21 Ⓐ Ⓑ Ⓒ Ⓓ Ⓔ	21 Ⓐ Ⓑ Ⓒ Ⓓ Ⓔ
22 Ⓐ Ⓑ Ⓒ Ⓓ Ⓔ	22 Ⓐ Ⓑ Ⓒ Ⓓ Ⓔ	22 Ⓐ Ⓑ Ⓒ Ⓓ Ⓔ	22 Ⓐ Ⓑ Ⓒ Ⓓ Ⓔ	22 Ⓐ Ⓑ Ⓒ Ⓓ Ⓔ
23 Ⓐ Ⓑ Ⓒ Ⓓ Ⓔ	23 Ⓐ Ⓑ Ⓒ Ⓓ Ⓔ	23 Ⓐ Ⓑ Ⓒ Ⓓ Ⓔ	23 Ⓐ Ⓑ Ⓒ Ⓓ Ⓔ	23 Ⓐ Ⓑ Ⓒ Ⓓ Ⓔ
24 Ⓐ Ⓑ Ⓒ Ⓓ Ⓔ	24 Ⓐ Ⓑ Ⓒ Ⓓ Ⓔ	24 Ⓐ Ⓑ Ⓒ Ⓓ Ⓔ	24 Ⓐ Ⓑ Ⓒ Ⓓ Ⓔ	24 Ⓐ Ⓑ Ⓒ Ⓓ Ⓔ
25 Ⓐ Ⓑ Ⓒ Ⓓ Ⓔ	25 Ⓐ Ⓑ Ⓒ Ⓓ Ⓔ	25 Ⓐ Ⓑ Ⓒ Ⓓ Ⓔ	25 Ⓐ Ⓑ Ⓒ Ⓓ Ⓔ	25 Ⓐ Ⓑ Ⓒ Ⓓ Ⓔ
26 Ⓐ Ⓑ Ⓒ Ⓓ Ⓔ	26 Ⓐ Ⓑ Ⓒ Ⓓ Ⓔ	26 Ⓐ Ⓑ Ⓒ Ⓓ Ⓔ	26 Ⓐ Ⓑ Ⓒ Ⓓ Ⓔ	26 Ⓐ Ⓑ Ⓒ Ⓓ Ⓔ
27 Ⓐ Ⓑ Ⓒ Ⓓ Ⓔ	27 Ⓐ Ⓑ Ⓒ Ⓓ Ⓔ	27 Ⓐ Ⓑ Ⓒ Ⓓ Ⓔ	27 Ⓐ Ⓑ Ⓒ Ⓓ Ⓔ	27 Ⓐ Ⓑ Ⓒ Ⓓ Ⓔ
28 Ⓐ Ⓑ Ⓒ Ⓓ Ⓔ	28 Ⓐ Ⓑ Ⓒ Ⓓ Ⓔ	28 Ⓐ Ⓑ Ⓒ Ⓓ Ⓔ	28 Ⓐ Ⓑ Ⓒ Ⓓ Ⓔ	28 Ⓐ Ⓑ Ⓒ Ⓓ Ⓔ
29 Ⓐ Ⓑ Ⓒ Ⓓ Ⓔ	29 Ⓐ Ⓑ Ⓒ Ⓓ Ⓔ	29 Ⓐ Ⓑ Ⓒ Ⓓ Ⓔ	29 Ⓐ Ⓑ Ⓒ Ⓓ Ⓔ	29 Ⓐ Ⓑ Ⓒ Ⓓ Ⓔ
30 Ⓐ Ⓑ Ⓒ Ⓓ Ⓔ	30 Ⓐ Ⓑ Ⓒ Ⓓ Ⓔ	30 Ⓐ Ⓑ Ⓒ Ⓓ Ⓔ	30 Ⓐ Ⓑ Ⓒ Ⓓ Ⓔ	30 Ⓐ Ⓑ Ⓒ Ⓓ Ⓔ

14 PLEASE PRINT INFORMATION

LAST NAME

FIRST NAME

DATE OF BIRTH

THE PREPTEST

- Logical Reasoning ....SECTION I

- Analytical Reasoning......................................SECTION II

- Logical Reasoning ....SECTION III

- Reading Comprehension...............................SECTION IV

- Writing Sample Materials

SECTION I

Time—35 minutes

25 Questions

Directions: The questions in this section are based on the reasoning contained in brief statements or passages. For some questions, more than one of the choices could conceivably answer the question. However, you are to choose the best answer; that is, the response that most accurately and completely answers the question. You should not make assumptions that are by commonsense standards implausible, superfluous, or incompatible with the passage. After you have chosen the best answer, blacken the corresponding space on your answer sheet.

1. Several years ago, most of one country's large banks failed and were taken over by a government agency. The agency is now selling these banks, aiming to strengthen the banking system in the process. But the banking system will not be strengthened if the former owners of these banks buy them back. So the agency is unlikely to achieve its goal, since _____.

The conclusion of the argument is properly drawn if which one of the following completes the passage?

(A) the agency may be unable to sell some of the banks

(B) a single company could buy more than one of the banks

(C) the country's overall economy is not much stronger than it was when the large banks failed

(D) the banks sold by the agency will be financially weaker than the country's other banks for some time

(E) all of the bidders for the banks are their former owners

2. Accountant: The newspaper industry habitually cites the rising cost of newsprint to explain falling profits. But when corrected for inflation, the cost of newsprint is no more than it was ten years ago. Far from being victims of high costs, newspapers have been benefiting from cheap newsprint for decades. The real threats to their profitability are falling circulation and falling advertising.

The accountant's argument proceeds by

(A) reinterpreting a popular analogy in order to use that analogy to support an alternative conclusion

(B) using economic data to raise doubts about the current effectiveness of a historically accepted approach

(C) criticizing a newly developed method by demonstrating that a conventional method shows better results

(D) challenging an explanation that has been given for a phenomenon in order to introduce a different explanation

(E) calling into question a justification for a practice by showing how the same justification can be used to support a clearly undesirable practice

3. Peter: Recent evidence suggests that moderate alcohol consumption has certain beneficial effects on health. In particular, alcohol creates an inhospitable environment in the human body for certain bacteria that can cause illness. Thus, alcohol consumption is, on balance, beneficial.

Which one of the following most accurately expresses a flaw in the reasoning in Peter's argument?

(A) It takes for granted that people choose to consume alcohol because they believe it is beneficial to their health.

(B) It draws a comparison based on popular belief rather than on scientific opinion.

(C) It fails to consider methods of achieving the same beneficial effects that do not involve alcohol.

(D) It draws a conclusion about alcohol consumption in general from a premise about moderate alcohol consumption.

(E) It fails to consider that alcohol may have no effect on many bacteria that cause illness in human beings.

GO ON TO THE NEXT PAGE.

4. Consultant: Children taught using innovative new educational methods learn to think more creatively than children taught using rote methods such as drills, but they are less adept at memorizing large amounts of information. Most jobs at Grodex Corporation require the ability to think creatively but do not require a strong ability to memorize. So Grodex should probably conduct its employee-training seminars using the innovative methods, because _____ .

Which one of the following most logically completes the consultant's argument?

(A) most of the employees at Grodex began in high school to learn the creative thinking skills that they later used on the job

(B) corporations that conduct training seminars for employees using innovative educational methods are generally more successful than are corporations that do not conduct training seminars

(C) less than half of the employees at Grodex regularly attend the company's training seminars

(D) the effects of teaching methods in the education of adults are generally very similar to the effects of those methods in the education of children

(E) knowing how to think creatively helps people to compensate for deficiencies in memorization skills

5. Essayist: If Earth's population continues to grow geometrically, then in a few centuries there will be ten people for every square meter (approximately one person per square foot) of Earth's surface. Some people have claimed that this will probably not be a problem, since humans will have learned by then how to colonize other planets. This would, however, be a temporary solution at best: if the population continues to double every 30 years, and if in the year 2500 half of Earth's population emigrated to Mars, then by the year 2530 Earth would be just as crowded as it had been before the emigration.

Which one of the following most accurately expresses the conclusion drawn in the essayist's argument?

(A) If Earth's population continues to grow geometrically, then in a few centuries the population density of Earth's surface will be ten people per square meter.

(B) Due to the continuing geometric growth of Earth's population, the problem of overpopulation of Earth will probably persist.

(C) If Earth's population continues to double every 30 years, and if at some point half of the population of Earth emigrated elsewhere, then after 30 years Earth would be just as crowded as it had been before the emigration.

(D) The population of Earth's surface will probably continue to grow geometrically even if temporary solutions to population growth, such as colonizing other planets, are adopted.

(E) Learning how to colonize other planets would, at best, be a temporary solution to the overcrowding of Earth.

6. A recent taste test reveals that most people like low-fat chocolate ice cream as much as its full-fat counterpart. Previous tests with vanilla ice cream found that people tended to dislike low-fat versions, complaining of a harsher taste. Chemists point out that chocolate is a very complex flavor, requiring around 500 distinct chemical compounds to produce it. Hence, this complexity probably masks any difference in taste due to the lack of fat.

Which one of the following, if true, most strengthens the argument?

(A) Most people prefer full-fat chocolate ice cream to full-fat vanilla ice cream.

(B) The subjects of the previous tests were not informed of the difference in fat content.

(C) The more distinct compounds required to produce a flavor, the better people like it.

(D) Vanilla is known to be a significantly less complex flavor than chocolate.

(E) Most people are aware of the chemical complexities of different flavors.

GO ON TO THE NEXT PAGE.

7. Ethicist: Robert Gillette has argued that because a thorough knowledge of genetics would enable us to cure the over 3,000 inherited disorders that affect humanity, deciphering the human genetic code will certainly benefit humanity despite its enormous cost. Gillette's argument is not persuasive, however, because he fails to consider that such knowledge might ultimately harm human beings more than it would benefit them.

Which one of the following most accurately expresses the conclusion of the ethicist's argument?

(A) Gillette's argument wrongly assumes that deciphering the genetic code will lead to cures for genetic disorders.
(B) Deciphering the genetic code might ultimately harm human beings more than benefit them.
(C) Because of its possible negative consequences, genetic research should not be conducted.
(D) Gillette's claim that a thorough knowledge of genetics would enable us to cure over 3,000 disorders is overstated.
(E) Gillette's argument is unconvincing because it ignores certain possible consequences of genetic research.

8. Many uses have been claimed for hypnosis, from combating drug addiction to overcoming common phobias. A recent experimental study helps illuminate the supposed connection between hypnosis and increased power of recall. A number of subjects listened to a long, unfamiliar piece of instrumental music. Under subsequent hypnosis, half the subjects were asked to recall salient passages from the musical piece and half were asked to describe scenes from "the film they had just viewed," despite their not having just seen a film. The study found that the subjects in the second group were equally confident and detailed in their movie recollections as the subjects in the first group were in their music recollections.

Which one of the following statements is most supported by the information above?

(A) Many of the claims made on behalf of hypnosis are overstated.
(B) Hypnosis cannot significantly increase a person's power of recall.
(C) Recalling events under hypnosis inevitably results in false memories.
(D) What people recall under hypnosis depends to at least some extent on suggestion.
(E) Visual memory is enhanced more by hypnosis than is auditory memory.

9. Records from 1850 to 1900 show that in a certain region, babies' birth weights each year varied with the success of the previous year's crops: the more successful the crops, the higher the birth weights. This indicates that the health of a newborn depends to a large extent on the amount of food available to the mother during her pregnancy.

The argument proceeds by

(A) inferring from a claimed correlation between two phenomena that two other phenomena are causally connected to one another
(B) inferring from the claim that two phenomena have fluctuated together that one of those phenomena must be the sole cause of the other
(C) inferring from records concerning a past correlation between two phenomena that that correlation still exists
(D) inferring from records concerning two phenomena the existence of a common cause of the phenomena and then presenting a hypothesis about that common cause
(E) inferring the existence of one causal connection from that of another and then providing an explanation for the existence of the two causal connections

10. Vincent: No scientific discipline can study something that cannot be measured, and since happiness is an entirely subjective experience, it cannot be measured.

Yolanda: Just as optometry relies on patients' reports of what they see, happiness research relies on subjects' reports of how they feel. Surely optometry is a scientific discipline.

Vincent's and Yolanda's statements provide the most support for concluding that they disagree over which one of the following?

(A) Happiness is an entirely subjective experience.
(B) Optometry is a scientific discipline.
(C) A scientific discipline can rely on subjective reports.
(D) Happiness research is as much a scientific discipline as optometry is.
(E) Experiences that cannot be measured are entirely subjective experiences.

GO ON TO THE NEXT PAGE.

11. Although large cities are generally more polluted than the countryside, increasing urbanization may actually reduce the total amount of pollution generated nationwide. Residents of large cities usually rely more on mass transportation and live in smaller, more energy-efficient dwellings than do people in rural areas. Thus, a given number of people will produce less pollution if concentrated in a large city than if dispersed among many small towns.

Which one of the following most accurately describes the role played in the argument by the claim that increasing urbanization may actually reduce the total amount of pollution generated nationwide?

(A) It is used to support the conclusion that people should live in large cities.

(B) It is a statement offered to call into question the claim that large cities are generally more polluted than the countryside.

(C) It is a statement serving merely to introduce the topic to be addressed in the argument and plays no logical role.

(D) It is a premise offered in support of the conclusion that large cities are generally more polluted than the countryside.

(E) It is a claim that the rest of the argument is designed to establish.

12. Climatologist: Over the coming century, winter temperatures are likely to increase in the Rocky Mountains due to global warming. This will cause a greater proportion of precipitation to fall as rain instead of snow. Therefore, the mountain snowpack will probably melt more rapidly and earlier in the season, leading to greater spring flooding and less storable water to meet summer demands.

Which one of the following, if true, most strengthens the climatologist's argument?

(A) Global warming will probably cause a substantial increase in the average amount of annual precipitation in the Rocky Mountains over the coming century.

(B) In other mountainous regions after relatively mild winters, the melting of snowpacks has led to greater spring flooding and less storable water, on average, than in those mountainous regions after colder winters.

(C) On average, in areas of the Rocky Mountains in which winters are relatively mild, there is less storable water to meet summer demands than there is in areas of the Rocky Mountains that experience colder winters.

(D) On average, in the regions of the world with the mildest winters, there is more spring flooding and less storable water than in regions of the world with much colder winters.

(E) The larger a mountain snowpack is, the greater the amount of spring flooding it is likely to be responsible for producing.

13. Animal feed should not include genetically modified plants. A study found that laboratory rats fed genetically modified potatoes for 30 days tended to develop intestinal deformities and a weakened immune system, whereas rats fed a normal diet of foods that were not genetically modified did not develop these problems.

Which one of the following, if true, most weakens the argument?

(A) Potatoes are not normally a part of the diet of laboratory rats.

(B) The rats tended to eat more of the genetically modified potatoes at the beginning of the 30 days than they did toward the end of the 30 days.

(C) Intestinal deformities at birth are not uncommon among rats bred in laboratory conditions.

(D) Genetically modified potatoes have the same nutritional value to rats as do potatoes that are not genetically modified.

(E) The researchers conducting the study were unable to explain how the genetic modifications of the potatoes would have caused the intestinal deformities or a weakened immune system in the rats.

GO ON TO THE NEXT PAGE.

14. Some philosophers explain visual perception by suggesting that when we visually perceive an object, a mental image of that object forms in our mind. However, this hypothesis cannot be correct, since it would require an inner self visually perceiving the newly formed mental image; this would in turn require that the inner self have a mental image of that mental image, and so on. But such an infinite regress is absurd.

Which one of the following arguments is most similar in its pattern of reasoning to the argument above?

(A) According to some linguists, many of the world's languages can be traced back to a common source known as Indo-European. However, Indo-European cannot be the earliest language, for if it were, then there would be no language from which it was derived. But this is highly unlikely, given the overwhelming evidence that humans spoke long before the advent of Indo-European.

(B) The claim that any scientific theory is adequate as long as it agrees with all the empirical data cannot be correct. For there are an infinite number of theories all of which account equally well for the empirical data, and they cannot all be true at the same time.

(C) Some historians claim that no theory is ever genuinely new; no matter how clever a theory is, there is always a precedent theory that contains its gist. But if this were true, then every theory would have a precedent theory containing its gist, and this precedent theory would also have a precedent theory, and so on, without end. Since this is clearly impossible, the historians' claim must be false.

(D) Some engineers define a structure's foundation as that part of the structure that supports the rest of the structure. This definition is unfortunate, however, because it evokes the suggestion that the foundation itself does not have any support, which, of course, is absurd.

(E) Some people claim that the first library was the library of Alexandria, which for many centuries contained the largest collection of books in the world. However, Alexandria's collection was itself put together from smaller collections, small libraries in themselves. It follows that the library of Alexandria was not the first in the world.

15. Greatly exceeding the recommended daily intake of vitamins A and D is dangerous, for they can be toxic at high levels. For some vitamin-fortified foods, each serving, as defined by the manufacturer, has 100 percent of the recommended daily intake of these vitamins. But many people overestimate what counts as a standard serving of vitamin-fortified foods such as cereal, consuming two to three times what the manufacturers define as standard servings.

Which one of the following is most strongly supported by the information above?

(A) Few people who consume vitamin-fortified foods are aware of the recommended daily intake of vitamins A and D.

(B) Some people who consume vitamin-fortified foods exceed the recommended daily intake of vitamins A and D.

(C) Some people mistakenly believe it is healthy to consume more than the recommended daily intake of vitamins A and D.

(D) Most people who eat vitamin-fortified foods should not take any vitamin supplements.

(E) Manufacturers are unaware that many people consume vitamin-fortified foods in amounts greater than the standard serving sizes.

GO ON TO THE NEXT PAGE.

16. At the end of 1997 several nations stated that their oil reserves had not changed since the end of 1996. But oil reserves gradually drop as old oil fields are drained and rise suddenly as new oil fields are discovered. Therefore, oil reserves are unlikely to remain unchanged from one year to the next. So most of the nations stating that their oil reserves were unchanged are probably incorrect.

Which one of the following is an assumption the argument requires?

(A)   For any nation with oil reserves, it is more likely that the nation was mistaken in its statements about changes in its oil reserves than that the nation's oil reserves remained unchanged.

(B)   It is likely that in 1997, in most of the nations that stated that their oil reserves were unchanged, old oil fields were drained or new oil fields were discovered, or both.

(C)   During the course of 1997, the oil reserves of at least one nation not only gradually dropped but also rose suddenly.

(D)   If a nation incorrectly stated at the end of 1997 that its oil reserves had not changed since the end of 1996, then during 1997 that nation drained its old oil fields and discovered new ones.

(E)   If a nation's oil reserves change from one year to the next, then that nation is obligated to report the change correctly.

17. If a motor is sound-insulated, then it is quiet enough to use in home appliances. If a motor is quiet enough to use in home appliances, then it can be used in institutional settings. None of the motors manufactured by EM Industries are quiet enough to use in home appliances.

If the statements above are true, which one of the following must be true?

(A)   If a motor can be used in institutional settings, then it is sound-insulated.

(B)   None of the motors manufactured by EM Industries are sound-insulated.

(C)   At least some of the motors manufactured by EM Industries can be used in institutional settings.

(D)   If a motor is quiet enough to use in home appliances, then it is sound-insulated.

(E)   None of the motors manufactured by EM Industries can be used in institutional settings.

18. Mayor: A huge protest against plans to build a chemical plant in this town was held yesterday. The protesters claim that the factory could cause health problems. But this worry can be dismissed. Most of the protesters were there only because they were paid to show up by property developers who are concerned that the factory would lower the value of nearby land that they own.

Which one of the following most accurately expresses a flaw in reasoning in the mayor's argument?

(A)   The argument mischaracterizes an opposing view and then attacks this mischaracterized view.

(B)   The argument attempts to persuade by inducing fear of the consequences of rejecting its conclusion.

(C)   The argument rejects a claim simply because of the motivation that some people have for making it.

(D)   The argument generalizes on the basis of a few unrepresentative cases.

(E)   The argument mistakes a claim that a result is possible for a claim that the result is inevitable.

19. One should not intentionally misrepresent another person's beliefs unless one's purpose in doing so is to act in the interest of that other person.

Which one of the following actions most clearly violates the principle stated?

(A)   Ann told someone that Bruce thought the Apollo missions to the moon were elaborate hoaxes, even though she knew he did not think this; she did so merely to make him look ridiculous.

(B)   Claude told someone that Thelma believed in extraterrestrial beings, even though he knew she believed no such thing; he did so solely to keep this other person from bothering her.

(C)   In Maria's absence John had told people that Maria believed that university education should be free of charge. He knew that Maria would not want him telling people this, but he wanted these people to think highly of Maria.

(D)   Harvey told Josephine that he thought Josephine would someday be famous. Harvey did not really think that Josephine would ever be famous, but he said she would because he thought she would like him as a result.

(E)   Wanda told people that George thought Egypt is in Asia. Wanda herself knew that Egypt is in Africa, but she told people that George thought it was in Asia because she wanted people to know that George knew little about geography.

20. Adjusted for inflation, the income earned from wool sales by a certain family of Australian sheep farmers grew substantially during the period from 1840 to 1860. This is because the price for wool sold on the international market was higher than the price paid on domestic markets and the percentage and amount of its wool that this family sold internationally increased dramatically during that period. But even though the family generated more income from selling their wool, they failed to enjoy a commensurate increase in prosperity.

Which one of the following would, if true, help most to resolve the apparent paradox described above?

(A) At the end of the 1800s, prices in general in Australia rose more rapidly than did the wholesale price of wool sold domestically.

(B) The prices of wool sold to domestic markets by Australian sheep farmers decreased dramatically during the period in question.

(C) The international and domestic prices for mutton, sheepskins, and certain other products produced by all Australian sheep farmers fell sharply during the period in question.

(D) Competition in wool sales increased during the period in question, leaving Australian wool producers in a less favorable position than previously.

(E) Among Australian sheep farmers, the percentage who made their living exclusively from international wool sales increased significantly during the period in question.

21. Lawyer: If you take something that you have good reason to think is someone else's property, that is stealing, and stealing is wrong. However, Meyers had no good reason to think that the compost in the public garden was anyone else's property, so it was not wrong for Meyers to take it.

The reasoning in the lawyer's argument is flawed in that the argument

(A) confuses a factual claim with a moral judgment

(B) takes for granted that Meyers would not have taken the compost if he had good reason to believe that it was someone else's property

(C) takes a condition that by itself is enough to make an action wrong to also be necessary in order for the action to be wrong

(D) fails to consider the possibility that the compost was Meyers' property

(E) concludes that something is certainly someone else's property when there is merely good, but not conclusive, reason to think that it is someone else's property

22. From time to time there is a public outcry against predatory pricing—where a company deliberately sells its products at prices low enough to drive its competitors out of business. But this practice clearly should be acceptable, because even after its competitors go out of business, the mere threat of renewed competition will prevent the company from raising its prices to unreasonable levels.

Which one of the following is an assumption on which the argument depends?

(A) Any company that is successful will inevitably induce competitors to enter the market.

(B) It is unlikely that several competing companies will engage in predatory pricing simultaneously.

(C) Only the largest and wealthiest companies can engage in predatory pricing for a sustained period of time.

(D) It is only competition or the threat of competition that keeps companies from raising prices.

(E) Any pricing practice that does not result in unreasonable prices should be acceptable.

23. If the prosecutor wanted to charge Frank with embezzlement, then Frank would already have been indicted. But Frank has not been indicted. So clearly Frank is not an embezzler.

The flawed pattern of reasoning exhibited by which one of the following is most similar to that exhibited by the argument above?

(A) If Rosita knew that her 9:00 appointment would cancel, she would not come in to work until 10:00. She did not come in until 10:00. So she must have known her 9:00 appointment would cancel.

(B) If Barry had won the lottery, he would stay home to celebrate. But Barry did not win the lottery, so he will be in to work today.

(C) If Makoto believed that he left the oven on, he would rush home. But Makoto is still at work. So obviously he did not leave the oven on.

(D) If Tamara believed she was getting a promotion, she would come in to work early. She did come in early. So apparently she is getting a promotion.

(E) If Lucy believed she was going to be fired, she would not come in to work today. She is going to be fired, so clearly she will not be coming in today.

GO ON TO THE NEXT PAGE.

24. Pediatrician: Swollen tonsils give rise to breathing problems during sleep, and the surgical removal of children's swollen tonsils has been shown to alleviate sleep disturbances. So removing children's tonsils before swelling even occurs will ensure that the children do not experience any breathing problems during sleep.

The pediatrician's argument is most vulnerable to the criticism that it

(A) relies on an inappropriate appeal to authority

(B) relies on an assumption that is tantamount to assuming that the conclusion is true

(C) infers from the fact that an action has a certain effect that the action is intended to produce that effect

(D) fails to consider the possibility that there may be other medical reasons for surgically removing a child's tonsils

(E) fails to consider the possibility that some breathing problems during sleep may be caused by something other than swollen tonsils

25. It is unethical for government officials to use their knowledge of impending policies to financially benefit themselves if that knowledge is not available to the general public.

Which one of the following actions would be unethical according to the principle stated above?

(A) A company whose former manager is now an official with the Department of Natural Resources was one of several bidders for an extremely lucrative contract with the department; the names of the bidders were not disclosed to the public.

(B) A retired high-ranking military officer now owns a company that contracts with the Department of Defense. He uses his contacts with department officials to help his company obtain contracts.

(C) After a tax reform law was enacted, an official with the government's revenue agency obtained a 20 percent reduction in personal income tax by setting up tax shelters that were allowed by the new law.

(D) A Finance Department official, one of the few people who knew of a plan to tax luxury cars, bought a luxury car just before the plan was announced to the public in order to avoid paying the tax.

(E) An official with a government agency that regulates securities sold her stock in Acme just after she announced to the public that her agency was investigating Acme for improper accounting.

S T O P

IF YOU FINISH BEFORE TIME IS CALLED, YOU MAY CHECK YOUR WORK ON THIS SECTION ONLY.
DO NOT WORK ON ANY OTHER SECTION IN THE TEST.

SECTION II

Time—35 minutes

23 Questions

Directions: Each group of questions in this section is based on a set of conditions. In answering some of the questions, it may be useful to draw a rough diagram. Choose the response that most accurately and completely answers each question and blacken the corresponding space on your answer sheet.

Questions 1–5

A movie studio is scheduling the release of six films—*Fiesta, Glaciers, Hurricanes, Jets, Kangaroos,* and *Lovebird*. No two of these films can be released on the same date. The release schedule is governed by the following conditions:

    Fiesta must be released earlier than both *Jets* and
      Lovebird.
    Kangaroos must be released earlier than *Jets*, and *Jets*
      must be released earlier than *Hurricanes*.
    Lovebird must be released earlier than *Glaciers*.

1. Which one of the following CANNOT be true?

  (A)   *Fiesta* is released second.
  (B)   *Glaciers* is released third.
  (C)   *Hurricanes* is released fourth.
  (D)   *Kangaroos* is released fourth.
  (E)   *Kangaroos* is released fifth.

GO ON TO THE NEXT PAGE.

2. Which one of the following must be true?

(A)   *Fiesta* is released earlier than *Hurricanes*.
(B)   *Jets* is released earlier than *Glaciers*.
(C)   *Kangaroos* is released earlier than *Glaciers*.
(D)   *Lovebird* is released earlier than *Hurricanes*.
(E)   *Lovebird* is released earlier than *Jets*.

3. If *Glaciers* is released earlier than *Hurricanes*, then each of the following could be true EXCEPT:

(A)   *Glaciers* is released fourth.
(B)   *Jets* is released third.
(C)   *Kangaroos* is released second.
(D)   *Lovebird* is released third.
(E)   *Lovebird* is released fifth.

4. If *Lovebird* is released earlier than *Kangaroos*, which one of the following could be true?

(A)   *Lovebird* is released third.
(B)   *Lovebird* is released fourth.
(C)   *Hurricanes* is released earlier than *Lovebird*.
(D)   *Jets* is released earlier than *Glaciers*.
(E)   *Jets* is released earlier than *Lovebird*.

5. Which one of the following, if substituted for the condition that *Fiesta* must be released earlier than both *Jets* and *Lovebird*, would have the same effect on the order in which the films are released?

(A)   Only *Kangaroos* can be released earlier than *Fiesta*.
(B)   *Kangaroos* must be released earlier than *Lovebird*.
(C)   *Fiesta* must be released either first or second.
(D)   *Fiesta* must be released earlier than both *Kangaroos* and *Lovebird*.
(E)   Either *Fiesta* or *Kangaroos* must be released first.

GO ON TO THE NEXT PAGE.

Questions 6–11

The applications of seven job candidates—Farrell, Grant, Hong, Inman, Kent, Lopez, and Madsen—will be evaluated by four human resource officers—Rao, Smith, Tipton, and Ullman. Each application will be evaluated by exactly one officer, and each officer will evaluate at least one application, subject to the following constraints:

Grant's application must be evaluated by Ullman.

Farrell's application must be evaluated by the same officer who evaluates Lopez's application.

Neither Hong's application nor Madsen's application can be evaluated by the same officer who evaluates Inman's application.

The officer who evaluates Kent's application cannot evaluate any other applications.

Smith must evaluate more of the applications than Tipton does.

6. Which one of the following could be the assignment of applications to officers?

(A) Rao: Hong
Smith: Farrell, Lopez, Madsen
Tipton: Kent
Ullman: Grant, Inman

(B) Rao: Inman
Smith: Hong, Lopez, Madsen
Tipton: Kent
Ullman: Farrell, Grant

(C) Rao: Madsen
Smith: Farrell, Lopez
Tipton: Kent
Ullman: Grant, Hong, Inman

(D) Rao: Farrell, Lopez
Smith: Hong, Kent, Madsen
Tipton: Inman
Ullman: Grant

(E) Rao: Farrell, Grant, Lopez
Smith: Hong, Madsen
Tipton: Kent
Ullman: Inman

GO ON TO THE NEXT PAGE.

7. If Hong's application is evaluated by Rao, which one of the following could be true?

 (A) Farrell's application is evaluated by Rao.
 (B) Inman's application is evaluated by Smith.
 (C) Kent's application is evaluated by Rao.
 (D) Lopez's application is evaluated by Ullman.
 (E) Madsen's application is evaluated by Tipton.

8. If exactly two of the applications are evaluated by Tipton, then each of the following must be true EXCEPT:

 (A) Exactly one of the applications is evaluated by Rao.
 (B) Exactly one of the applications is evaluated by Ullman.
 (C) Farrell's application is evaluated by Tipton.
 (D) Inman's application is evaluated by Smith.
 (E) Lopez's application is evaluated by Smith.

9. If the officer who evaluates Madsen's application does not evaluate any other application, which one of the following must be true?

 (A) Madsen's application is evaluated by Tipton.
 (B) Lopez's application is evaluated by Smith.
 (C) Kent's application is evaluated by Tipton.
 (D) Inman's application is evaluated by Smith.
 (E) Hong's application is evaluated by Smith.

10. If Farrell's application is evaluated by the same officer who evaluates Inman's application, then any of the following could be true EXCEPT:

 (A) Hong's application is evaluated by Ullman.
 (B) Kent's application is evaluated by Tipton.
 (C) Lopez's application is evaluated by Ullman.
 (D) Madsen's application is evaluated by Smith.
 (E) Madsen's application is evaluated by Ullman.

11. If Farrell's application is evaluated by Rao, then for how many of the other applications is the identity of the officer who evaluates it fully determined?

 (A) one
 (B) two
 (C) three
 (D) four
 (E) five

GO ON TO THE NEXT PAGE.

Questions 12–16

A six-week literature course is being planned in which six books—F, K, N, O, R, and T—will be discussed. The books will be discussed one at a time, one book per week. In addition, written summaries will be required for one or more of the books. The order in which the books are discussed and the selection of books to be summarized is subject to the following conditions:

No two books that are summarized are discussed in consecutive weeks.

If N is not summarized, then both R and T are summarized.

N is discussed earlier than T, and T is discussed earlier than O.

F is discussed earlier than O, and O is discussed earlier than both K and R.

12. Which one of the following could be the plan for the course, showing the order, from first to last, in which the books are discussed and the choice of books to be summarized?

(A) F, N, T, O, R, K; with only T and R summarized

(B) F, T, N, O, K, R; with only N and K summarized

(C) N, F, T, O, K, R; with only T, O, and R summarized

(D) N, T, F, O, K, R; with only T and O summarized

(E) N, T, O, F, K, R; with only T and R summarized

GO ON TO THE NEXT PAGE.

13. If N is the second book discussed and it is not summarized, which one of the following could be true?

(A) F is summarized.
(B) K is summarized.
(C) O is summarized.
(D) T is discussed earlier than F.
(E) The third book discussed is not summarized.

14. If O is summarized, which one of the following CANNOT be true?

(A) F is the first book discussed.
(B) K is the sixth book discussed.
(C) F is summarized.
(D) K is not summarized.
(E) N is not summarized.

15. If neither of the last two books discussed is summarized, which one of the following could be true?

(A) K is summarized.
(B) O is summarized.
(C) R is summarized.
(D) F and T are summarized.
(E) N is not summarized.

16. Which one of the following, if substituted for the condition that F is discussed earlier than O, and O is discussed earlier than both K and R, would have the same effect in determining the plan for the literature course?

(A) T is discussed third, and the last two books discussed are K and R, not necessarily in that order.
(B) T is discussed earlier than F, and the last two books discussed are K and R, not necessarily in that order.
(C) K and R are among the last three books discussed, and F is among the first three books discussed.
(D) K and R are discussed in consecutive weeks, not necessarily in that order, and O is discussed fourth.
(E) K and R are discussed in consecutive weeks, not necessarily in that order, and F is discussed third.

GO ON TO THE NEXT PAGE.

Questions 17–23

A museum curator is arranging seven paintings—a Morisot, a Pissarro, a Renoir, a Sisley, a Turner, a Vuillard, and a Whistler. The paintings will be arranged in a horizontal row of seven positions, with the first position being closest to the entrance and the seventh being furthest from the entrance. The arrangement is subject to the following constraints:

  The Turner must be closer to the entrance than the Whistler is.

  The Renoir must be closer to the entrance than the Morisot is, with exactly one other painting between them.

  The Pissarro and the Sisley must be next to each other.

  If the Vuillard is not in the third position, it must be in the fourth position.

17. Which one of the following could be the arrangement of the paintings, listed in order from the first position to the seventh?

(A) Morisot, Turner, Renoir, Vuillard, Whistler, Sisley, Pissarro

(B) Pissarro, Sisley, Renoir, Vuillard, Morisot, Whistler, Turner

(C) Renoir, Turner, Morisot, Vuillard, Whistler, Sisley, Pissarro

(D) Sisley, Turner, Pissarro, Vuillard, Renoir, Whistler, Morisot

(E) Turner, Vuillard, Pissarro, Sisley, Renoir, Whistler, Morisot

GO ON TO THE NEXT PAGE.

18. If the Sisley is in the seventh position, which one of the following could be the position that the Turner is in?

   (A)   second
   (B)   third
   (C)   fourth
   (D)   fifth
   (E)   sixth

19. If the Pissarro is in the fifth position, which one of the following must be true?

   (A)   The Morisot is in the fourth position.
   (B)   The Renoir is in the second position.
   (C)   The Sisley is in the sixth position.
   (D)   The Turner is in the first position.
   (E)   The Vuillard is in the third position.

20. Any one of the following could be in the third position EXCEPT:

   (A)   the Morisot
   (B)   the Renoir
   (C)   the Sisley
   (D)   the Turner
   (E)   the Whistler

21. If the Renoir and the Morisot are both between the Turner and the Whistler, which one of the following could be true?

   (A)   The Pissarro is in the fifth position.
   (B)   The Sisley is in the second position.
   (C)   The Turner is in the third position.
   (D)   The Vuillard is in the fourth position.
   (E)   The Whistler is in the sixth position.

22. If there is exactly one painting between the Turner and the Whistler, which one of the following must be true?

   (A)   The Morisot is in the seventh position.
   (B)   The Pissarro is in the first position.
   (C)   The Renoir is in the fourth position.
   (D)   The Turner is in the second position.
   (E)   The Vuillard is in the third position.

23. If the Turner is next to the Vuillard, which one of the following is a pair of paintings in which the one mentioned first must be closer to the entrance than the one mentioned second?

   (A)   the Pissarro and the Sisley
   (B)   the Renoir and the Whistler
   (C)   the Turner and the Vuillard
   (D)   the Vuillard and the Turner
   (E)   the Whistler and the Renoir

S T O P

IF YOU FINISH BEFORE TIME IS CALLED, YOU MAY CHECK YOUR WORK ON THIS SECTION ONLY.
DO NOT WORK ON ANY OTHER SECTION IN THE TEST.

SECTION III
Time—35 minutes
26 Questions

Directions: The questions in this section are based on the reasoning contained in brief statements or passages. For some questions, more than one of the choices could conceivably answer the question. However, you are to choose the best answer; that is, the response that most accurately and completely answers the question. You should not make assumptions that are by commonsense standards implausible, superfluous, or incompatible with the passage. After you have chosen the best answer, blacken the corresponding space on your answer sheet.

1. Advertisement: GreenBank gives all of its customers unlimited free automatic teller machine (ATM) use. TekBank charges 25 cents for each ATM transaction. So, clearly, it costs more to bank at TekBank than at GreenBank.

    The reasoning in the advertisement's argument is misleading in that the argument

    (A) bases a recommendation solely on economic factors without considering whether other factors are more important
    (B) presents claims that are irrelevant to the issue under discussion in order to divert attention away from that issue
    (C) draws a conclusion about the overall cost of a service solely on the basis of a claim about the cost of one component of that service
    (D) concludes that a component of a service must have a property that the service as a whole possesses
    (E) concludes that a claim must be false because of the mere absence of evidence in its favor

2. Klein: The fact that the amount of matter that we have found in our galaxy is only one-tenth of what Einstein's theory predicts gives us good reason for abandoning his view.

    Brown: Given the great successes of Einstein's theory, it would be better to conclude that most of the matter in our galaxy has not yet been found.

    On the basis of their statements, Klein and Brown are committed to disagreeing over the truth of which one of the following statements?

    (A) Scientists have found only one-tenth of the matter that Einstein's theory predicts.
    (B) Einstein's theory has achieved many successes.
    (C) It is possible to determine the amount of matter in our galaxy without relying on Einstein's theory.
    (D) The failure to find all of the matter predicted by Einstein's theory should lead us to abandon it.
    (E) Scientists are able to accurately judge the amount of matter that has been found in our galaxy.

3. When chimpanzees become angry at other chimpanzees, they often engage in what primatologists call "threat gestures": grunting, spitting, or making abrupt, upsweeping arm movements. Chimpanzees also sometimes attack other chimpanzees out of anger. However, when they do attack, they almost never take time to make threat gestures first. And, conversely, threat gestures are rarely followed by physical attacks.

    Which one of the following, if true, most helps to explain the information about how often threat gestures are accompanied by physical attacks?

    (A) Chimpanzees engage in threat gestures when they are angry in order to preserve or enhance social status.
    (B) Making threat gestures helps chimpanzees vent aggressive feelings and thereby avoid physical aggression.
    (C) Threat gestures and physical attacks are not the only means by which chimpanzees display aggression.
    (D) Chimpanzees often respond to other chimpanzees' threat gestures with threat gestures of their own.
    (E) The chimpanzees that most often make threat gestures are the ones that least often initiate physical attacks.

GO ON TO THE NEXT PAGE.

4. The Magno-Blanket is probably able to relieve arthritic pain in older dogs. A hospital study of people suffering from severe joint pain found that 76 percent of those who were treated with magnets reported reduced pain after just 3 weeks. Dogs and humans have similar physiologies and the Magno-Blanket brings magnets into the same proximity to the dog's joints as they were to patients' joints in the hospital study.

Which one of the following, if true, most strengthens the argument?

(A) The Magno-Blanket is likely to be effective on cats and other pets as well if it is effective at reducing joint pain in arthritic dogs.

(B) Magnets have been shown to be capable of intensifying the transmission of messages from people's nerve cells to their brains.

(C) There are currently fewer means of safely alleviating arthritic pain in dogs than in humans.

(D) The patients in the hospital study suffering from severe joint pain who, after being treated with magnets, did not report reduced pain tended not to be those suffering from the most severe pain.

(E) Most of the patients in the hospital study suffering from severe joint pain who received a placebo rather than treatment with magnets did not report reduced pain.

5. Some people believe that advertising is socially pernicious—it changes consumers' preferences, thereby manipulating people into wanting things they would not otherwise want. However, classes in music and art appreciation change people's preferences for various forms of art and music, and there is nothing wrong with these classes. Therefore, _____.

Which one of the following most logically completes the argument?

(A) consumers would still want most of the things they want even if they were not advertised

(B) the social perniciousness of advertising is not limited to its effect on people's preferences

(C) the fact that advertising changes consumers' preferences does not establish that it is bad

(D) if advertising changes consumers' preferences, it generally does so in a positive way

(E) it is not completely accurate to say that advertising changes people's preferences

6. Many high school students interested in journalism think of journalism careers as involving glamorous international news gathering. But most journalists cover primarily local news, and the overwhelming majority of reporters work for local newspapers. Thus, high school career counselors should tell students who are interested in journalism what life is like for a typical reporter, that is, a reporter for a local newspaper.

Which one of the following principles would, if valid, most help to justify the reasoning above?

(A) High school students who have misconceptions about a career should not be encouraged to pursue that career.

(B) One should not encourage people to seek unattainable goals if one wishes to maximize those people's chances to lead happy lives.

(C) Students who are choosing a career should be encouraged to try to reach the top levels of that career.

(D) A career counselor should try to disabuse students of any unrealistic conceptions they may have about the likely consequences of choosing a particular career.

(E) Career counselors are not doing their job properly if they encourage people to make career choices that are initially appealing but that those people will later regret.

7. More pedestrian injuries occur at crosswalks marked by both striping on the roadway and flashing lights than occur at crosswalks not so marked. Obviously these so-called safety features are a waste of taxpayer money.

The reasoning in the argument is most vulnerable to criticism because the argument

(A) fails to consider that crosswalks marked by both striping and flashing lights are marked in this way precisely because they are the most dangerous ones

(B) takes for granted that safety features that fail to reduce the number of injuries are a waste of taxpayer money

(C) presumes that there are less expensive features that will reduce the number of pedestrian injuries just as effectively as striping and flashing lights

(D) takes for granted that crosswalks with both striping and flashing lights have no other safety features

(E) fails to consider that, in accidents involving pedestrians and cars, the injuries to pedestrians are nearly always more serious than the injuries to occupants of cars

GO ON TO THE NEXT PAGE.

8. John of Worcester, an English monk, recorded the sighting, on December 8, 1128, of two unusually large sunspots. Five days later a brilliant aurora borealis (northern lights) was observed in southern Korea. Sunspot activity is typically followed by the appearance of an aurora borealis, after a span of time that averages five days. Thus, the Korean sighting helps to confirm John of Worcester's sighting.

Which one of the following, if true, most strengthens the argument?

(A) An aurora borealis can sometimes occur even when there has been no significant sunspot activity in the previous week.

(B) Chinese sources recorded the sighting of sunspots more than 1000 years before John of Worcester did.

(C) Only heavy sunspot activity could have resulted in an aurora borealis viewable at a latitude as low as that of Korea.

(D) Because it is impossible to view sunspots with the naked eye under typical daylight conditions, the sighting recorded by John of Worcester would have taken place under unusual weather conditions such as fog or thin clouds.

(E) John of Worcester's account included a drawing of the sunspots, which could be the earliest illustration of sunspot activity.

9. Anyone believing that no individual can have an effect on society's future will as a result feel too helpless to act to change society for the better. Thus, anyone who wants to improve society should reject the belief that its future will be determined entirely by vast historical forces that individuals are powerless to change.

Which one of the following principles, if valid, most helps to justify the argument?

(A) Anyone who believes that individuals can have an effect on society's future should act to change society for the better.

(B) No one who rejects the belief that society's future will be determined by vast historical forces should believe that individuals cannot have an effect on it.

(C) Anyone who feels too helpless to act to change society for the better should reject the belief that its future will be determined by vast historical forces that individuals are powerless to change.

(D) No one who wants to improve society should accept any belief that makes him or her feel too helpless to act to change society for the better.

(E) Each individual should act to improve society if individuals in general feel powerless in the face of vast historical forces.

10. Company president: Whenever you subcontract the manufacturing of a product, you lose some control over the quality of that product. We do subcontract some manufacturing, but only with companies that maintain complete control over the quality of the products they supply.

Which one of the following can be properly inferred from the company president's statements?

(A) When the president's company subcontracts manufacturing of a product, it does not allow the subcontractor to further subcontract manufacturing of that product.

(B) Companies that subcontract the manufacturing of products are often disappointed in the quality of those products.

(C) The company president insists on having as much control as possible over the quality of the company's products.

(D) When consumers know that a product has been manufactured by a subcontractor, they are generally dubious about the product's quality.

(E) When a company manufactures some products in-house and subcontracts the manufacturing of others, the products made in-house will be of uniformly better quality.

11. Secondary school students achieve broad mastery of the curriculum if they are taught with methods appropriate to their learning styles and they devote significant effort to their studies. Thus, if such broad mastery is not achieved by the students in a particular secondary school, those students are not being taught with methods appropriate to their learning styles.

The conclusion can be properly drawn if which one of the following is assumed?

(A) As long as secondary school students are taught with methods appropriate to their learning styles, they will devote significant effort to their studies.

(B) Even if secondary school students are taught with methods appropriate to their learning styles, they will not achieve broad mastery of the curriculum if they do not devote significant effort to their studies.

(C) Secondary school students do not achieve broad mastery of the curriculum if they are not taught with methods appropriate to their learning styles.

(D) Teaching secondary school students with methods appropriate to their learning styles does not always result in broad mastery of the curriculum by those students.

(E) Secondary school students who devote significant effort to their studies do not always achieve broad mastery of the curriculum.

GO ON TO THE NEXT PAGE.

12. Consumer advocate: Even if one can of fruit or vegetables weighs more than another, the heavier can does not necessarily contain more food. Canned fruits and vegetables are typically packed in water, which can make up more than half the total weight of the can's contents. And nothing stops unscrupulous canning companies from including more water per can than others include.

Which one of the following most accurately expresses the conclusion drawn in the consumer advocate's argument?

(A) The heavier of two cans of fruit or vegetables does not necessarily contain more food than the lighter of the two cans contains.
(B) The weight of the water in a can of fruit or vegetables can be more than half the total weight of the can's contents.
(C) Nothing stops unscrupulous canning companies from including more water per can than others include.
(D) Some canning companies include less food in cans of a given weight than others include.
(E) The heavier of two cans of fruits or vegetables may include more water than the lighter of the two cans contains.

13. Several three-year-olds who had learned to count to ten were trying to learn their telephone numbers. Although each child was familiar with the names of all the digits, no child could remember his or her phone number. Their teacher then taught each child a song whose lyrics contained his or her phone number. By the end of the day the children could remember their telephone numbers.

The situation described above best illustrates which one of the following propositions?

(A) There are some things that children cannot learn without the aid of songs.
(B) Familiarity with a concept is not always sufficient for knowing the words used to express it.
(C) Mnemonic devices such as songs are better than any other method for memorizing numbers.
(D) Children can learn to count without understanding the meaning of numbers.
(E) Songs are useful in helping children remember the order in which familiar words occur.

14. Some theorists argue that literary critics should strive to be value-neutral in their literary criticism. These theorists maintain that by exposing the meaning of literary works without evaluating them, critics will enable readers to make their own judgments about the works' merits. But literary criticism cannot be completely value-neutral. Thus, some theorists are mistaken about what is an appropriate goal for literary criticism.

The argument's conclusion follows logically if which one of the following is assumed?

(A) Any critic who is able to help readers make their own judgments about literary works' merits should strive to produce value-neutral criticism.
(B) If it is impossible to produce completely value-neutral literary criticism, then critics should not even try to be value-neutral.
(C) Critics are more likely to provide criticisms of the works they like than to provide criticisms of the works they dislike.
(D) The less readers understand the meaning of a literary work, the less capable they will be of evaluating that work's merits.
(E) Critics who try to avoid rendering value judgments about the works they consider tend to influence readers' judgments less than other critics do.

GO ON TO THE NEXT PAGE.

15. Amoebas, like human beings, generally withdraw from stimuli that cause them physical damage. Humans do this because such stimuli cause them pain. Thus all microscopic organisms must also be capable of feeling pain.

Which one of the following exhibits flawed reasoning most similar to that exhibited by the argument above?

(A) Poets, like people under hypnosis, frequently use language in odd, incomprehensible ways. People under hypnosis do this because their inhibitions are lower than those of most people. Thus all artists must have lower inhibitions than most people have.

(B) Like nonprofit organizations, corporations usually provide some free public services. Nonprofit organizations do this solely because of their members' desire to make the world a better place. Thus this is probably also the main motive of most corporations.

(C) Most professional athletes practice regularly for the same reason. Professional boxers spend several hours a day practicing in order to excel in competition. Thus professional skaters probably also practice in order to excel in competition.

(D) Predatory birds, like many predatory animals, are generally solitary hunters. Some predatory mammals hunt alone because there is not enough food to support a pack of them in one area. Thus hawks, which are predatory birds, probably hunt alone.

(E) Hiking trails in British Columbia, like those in New Mexico, are concentrated in mountainous regions. In New Mexico this is partly because low-lying areas are too hot and arid for comfortable hiking. Thus hikers must also feel less comfortable hiking in low-lying areas of British Columbia.

16. Zoologist: In the Lake Champlain area, as the North American snowshoe hare population grows, so do the populations of its predators. As predator numbers increase, the hares seek food in more heavily forested areas, which contain less food, and so the hare population declines. Predator populations thus decline, the hare population starts to increase, and the cycle begins again. Yet these facts alone cannot explain why populations of snowshoe hares everywhere behave simultaneously in this cyclical way. Since the hare population cycle is well correlated with the regular cycle of sunspot activity, that activity is probably a causal factor as well.

Each of the following, if true, supports the zoologist's reasoning EXCEPT:

(A) Reproduction in predator populations increases when sunspot activity indirectly affects hormonal processes associated with reproduction.

(B) Local weather patterns that can affect species' population changes can occur both in the presence of sunspot activity and in its absence.

(C) Brighter light during sunspot activity subtly but significantly improves the ability of predators to detect and capture hares.

(D) The variation from cycle to cycle in the magnitude of the highs and lows in snowshoe hare populations is highly correlated with variations from cycle to cycle in the intensity of highs and lows in sunspot activity.

(E) Sunspot activity is correlated with increases and decreases in the nutritional value of vegetation eaten by the hares.

GO ON TO THE NEXT PAGE.

17. Science teacher: In any nation, a flourishing national scientific community is essential to a successful economy. For such a community to flourish requires that many young people become excited enough about science that they resolve to become professional scientists. Good communication between scientists and the public is necessary to spark that excitement.

The science teacher's statements provide the most support for which one of the following?

(A) If scientists communicate with the public, many young people will become excited enough about science to resolve to become professional scientists.

(B) The extent to which a national scientific community flourishes depends principally on the number of young people who become excited enough about science to resolve to become professional scientists.

(C) No nation can have a successful economy unless at some point scientists have communicated well with the public.

(D) It is essential to any nation's economy that most of the young people in that nation who are excited about science become professional scientists.

(E) An essential component of success in any scientific endeavor is good communication between the scientists involved in that endeavor and the public.

18. A recent magazine article argued that most companies that do not already own videoconferencing equipment would be wasting their money if they purchased it. However, this is clearly not true. In a recent survey of businesses that have purchased such equipment, most of the respondents stated that the videoconferencing equipment was well worth its cost.

The reasoning in the argument is flawed in that the argument

(A) concludes that something is worth its cost merely on the grounds that many businesses have purchased it

(B) takes a condition sufficient to justify purchasing costly equipment to be necessary in order for the cost of the purchase to be justified

(C) rejects a position merely on the grounds that an inadequate argument has been given for it

(D) relies on a sample that it is reasonable to suppose is unrepresentative of the group about which it draws its conclusion

(E) confuses the cost of an item with its value to the purchaser

19. Auditor: XYZ, a construction company, purchased 20 new trucks 3 years ago, and there is no record of any of those trucks being sold last year. Records indicate, however, that XYZ sold off all of its diesel-powered trucks last year. We can thus conclude that none of the 20 trucks purchased 3 years ago were diesel powered.

Which one of the following is an assumption required by the auditor's reasoning?

(A) All of the trucks that XYZ sold last year were diesel powered.

(B) XYZ did not purchase any used trucks 3 years ago.

(C) XYZ did not purchase any new trucks since it purchased the 20 trucks 3 years ago.

(D) None of the 20 trucks was sold before last year.

(E) XYZ no longer owns any trucks that it purchased more than 3 years ago.

20. Taylor: From observing close friends and relatives, it is clear to me that telepathy is indeed possible between people with close psychic ties. The amazing frequency with which a good friend or family member knows what one is thinking or feeling cannot be dismissed as mere coincidence.

Taylor's reasoning is most vulnerable to criticism on the grounds that it

(A) is based on too small a sample to yield a reliable conclusion

(B) fails to address a highly plausible alternative explanation for all instances of the observed phenomenon

(C) relies crucially on an illegitimate appeal to emotion

(D) presumes, without providing justification, that one can never know what a stranger is thinking or feeling

(E) appeals to a premise one would accept only if one already accepted the truth of the conclusion

GO ON TO THE NEXT PAGE.

3

21. Prolonged exposure to sulfur fumes permanently damages one's sense of smell. In one important study, 100 workers from sulfur-emitting factories and a control group of 100 workers from other occupations were asked to identify a variety of chemically reproduced scents, including those of foods, spices, and flowers. On average, the factory workers successfully identified 10 percent of the scents compared to 50 percent for the control group.

Each of the following, if true, weakens the argument EXCEPT:

(A) The chemicals used in the study closely but not perfectly reproduced the corresponding natural scents.

(B) The subjects in the study were tested in the environments where they usually work.

(C) Most members of the control group had participated in several earlier studies that involved the identification of scents.

(D) Every sulfur-emitting factory with workers participating in the study also emits other noxious fumes.

(E) Because of the factories' locations, the factory workers were less likely than those in the control group to have been exposed to many of the scents used in the study.

22. Principle: Anyone who has more than one overdue book out on loan from the library at the same time must be fined if some of the overdue books are not children's books and that person has previously been fined for overdue books.

Application: Since three of the books that Kessler currently has out on loan from the library are overdue, Kessler must be fined.

Which one of the following, if true, justifies the above application of the principle?

(A) Some of the books that Kessler currently has out on loan from the library are not children's books, and Kessler was fined last year for returning a children's book late.

(B) One of the overdue books that Kessler currently has out on loan from the library is a novel for adults, and Kessler was fined last year for returning this book late.

(C) None of the books that Kessler currently has out on loan from the library is a children's book and in previous years Kessler has returned various books late.

(D) Kessler was fined by the library several times in the past for overdue books, but none of the overdue books for which Kessler was fined were children's books.

(E) Kessler has never before been fined for overdue books, but the three overdue books that Kessler currently has out on loan from the library are months overdue.

23. Medical school professor: Most malpractice suits arise out of patients' perceptions that their doctors are acting negligently or carelessly. Many doctors now regard medicine as a science rather than an art, and are less compassionate as a result. Harried doctors sometimes treat patients rudely, discourage them from asking questions, or patronize them. Lawsuits could be avoided if doctors learned to listen better to patients. Unfortunately, certain economic incentives encourage doctors to treat patients rudely.

The medical school professor's statements, if true, most strongly support which one of the following?

(A) Economic incentives to treat patients rudely are the main cause of doctors being sued for malpractice.

(B) The economic incentives in the health care system encourage doctors to regard medicine as a science rather than as an art.

(C) Malpractice suits brought against doctors are, for the most part, unjustified.

(D) The scientific outlook in medicine should be replaced by an entirely different approach to medicine.

(E) Doctors foster, by their actions, the perception that they do not really care about their patients.

GO ON TO THE NEXT PAGE.

24. If the concrete is poured while the ground is wet, it will not form a solid foundation. If the concrete does not form a solid foundation, it will either settle unevenly or crack. So if the concrete settles evenly, either it was poured while the ground was dry or it will crack.

Which one of the following arguments is most closely parallel in its reasoning to the reasoning in the argument above?

(A) The film will not be properly exposed if the camera is not working properly. If the film is not properly exposed, then the photograph will be either blurred or dark. So if the photograph is not blurred, either the camera is working properly or the photograph will be dark.

(B) If the camera is working properly, the photograph will not be blurred. The photograph will be blurred if the film is either not properly exposed or not properly developed. So if the camera is working properly, the film will be both properly exposed and properly developed.

(C) The photograph will either be blurred or dark if the camera is not working properly. This photograph is not blurred, so if the photograph is not dark, the camera is working properly.

(D) If the camera is working properly, the film will be properly exposed. If either the film is properly exposed or corrections are made during the developing process, the photograph will not be dark. So if the camera is working properly, the photograph will not be dark.

(E) The camera will work properly only if the film is properly exposed. But the film cannot be properly exposed if there is either not enough or too much light. So the camera will not work properly if there is either too much or not enough light.

25. New evidence indicates that recent property development bordering a national park has not adversely affected the park's wildlife. On the contrary, a comparison of the most recent survey of the park's wildlife with one conducted just prior to the development shows that the amount of wildlife has in fact increased over the intervening decade. Moreover, the park's resources can support its current wildlife populations without strain.

Which one of the following, if true, most strengthens the argument?

(A) While both surveys found the same species of animals in the park, the more recent survey found greater numbers of animals belonging to each species.

(B) The more recent survey was taken in the summer, when the diversity of wildlife in the park is at its greatest.

(C) Migration of wildlife into the park from the adjacent developing areas has increased animal populations to levels beyond those that the resources of the park could have supported a decade ago.

(D) The most recent techniques for surveying wildlife are better at locating difficult-to-find animals than were older techniques.

(E) The more recent survey not only involved counting the animals found in the park but, unlike the earlier survey, also provided an inventory of the plant life found within the park.

26. As advances in medical research and technology have improved the ability of the medical profession to diagnose and treat a wide variety of illnesses and injuries, life spans have increased and overall health has improved. Yet, over the past few decades there has been a steady and significant increase in the rate of serious infections.

Which one of the following, if true, most helps to resolve the apparent discrepancy in the information above?

(A) It remains true that doctors sometimes prescribe ineffective medications due to misdiagnosis.

(B) Life spans have increased precisely because overall health has improved.

(C) The vast majority of serious infections are now curable, although many require hospitalization.

(D) As a population increases in size, there is a directly proportional increase in the number of serious infections.

(E) Modern treatments for many otherwise fatal illnesses increase the patient's susceptibility to infection.

S T O P

IF YOU FINISH BEFORE TIME IS CALLED, YOU MAY CHECK YOUR WORK ON THIS SECTION ONLY.
DO NOT WORK ON ANY OTHER SECTION IN THE TEST.

SECTION IV

Time—35 minutes

27 Questions

<u>Directions:</u> Each set of questions in this section is based on a single passage or a pair of passages. The questions are to be answered on the basis of what is <u>stated</u> or <u>implied</u> in the passage or pair of passages. For some of the questions, more than one of the choices could conceivably answer the question. However, you are to choose the <u>best</u> answer; that is, the response that most accurately and completely answers the question, and blacken the corresponding space on your answer sheet.

African American painter Sam Gilliam (b. 1933) is internationally recognized as one of the foremost painters associated with the Washington Color School, a group of Color Field style painters practicing in
(5) Washington, D.C. during the 1950s and 1960s. The Color Field style was an important development in abstract art that emerged after the rise of abstract expressionism. It evolved from complex and minimally representational abstractions in the 1950s to totally
(10) nonrepresentational, simplified works of bright colors in the 1960s.

Gilliam's participation in the Color Field movement was motivated in part by his reaction to the art of his African American contemporaries, much of which was
(15) strictly representational and was intended to convey explicit political statements. Gilliam found their approach to be aesthetically conservative: the message was unmistakable, he felt, and there was little room for the expression of subtlety or ambiguity or, more
(20) importantly, the exploration of new artistic territory through experimentation and innovation. For example, one of his contemporaries worked with collage, assembling disparate bits of images from popular magazines into loosely structured compositions that
(25) depicted the period's political issues—themes such as urban life, the rural South, and African American music. Though such art was quite popular with the general public, Gilliam was impatient with its straightforward, literal approach to representation.
(30) In its place he sought an artistic form that was more expressive than a painted figure or a political slogan, more evocative of the complexity of human experience in general, and of the African American experience in particular. In this he represented a view that was then
(35) rare among African American artists.

Gilliam's highly experimental paintings epitomized his refusal to conform to the public's expectation that African American artists produce explicitly political art. His early experiments included
(40) pouring paint onto stained canvases and folding canvases over onto themselves. Then around 1965 Gilliam became the first painter to introduce the idea of the unsupported canvas. Partially inspired by the sight of neighbors hanging laundry on clotheslines,
(45) Gilliam began to drape huge pieces of loose canvas along floors and fold them up and down walls, even suspending them from ceilings, giving them a third dimension and therefore a sculptural quality. These efforts demonstrate a sensitivity to the texture of daily
(50) experience, as well as the ability to generate tension by juxtaposing conceptual opposites—such as surface

and depth or chaos and control—to form a cohesive whole. In this way, Gilliam helped advance the notion that the deepest, hardest-to-capture emotions
(55) and tensions of being African American could not be represented directly, but were expressed more effectively through the creation of moods that would allow these emotions and tensions to be felt by all audiences.

1. In the passage, the author is primarily concerned with

(A) describing the motivation behind and nature of an artist's work
(B) describing the political themes that permeate an artist's work
(C) describing the evolution of an artist's style over a period of time
(D) demonstrating that a certain artist's views were rare among African American artists
(E) demonstrating that a certain artist was able to transcend his technical limitations

2. Which one of the following would come closest to exemplifying the characteristics of Gilliam's work as described in the passage?

(A) a brightly colored painting carefully portraying a man dressed in work clothes and holding a shovel in his hands
(B) a large, wrinkled canvas painted with soft, blended colors and overlaid with glued-on newspaper photographs depicting war scenes
(C) a painted abstract caricature of a group of jazz musicians waiting to perform
(D) a long unframed canvas painted with images of the sea and clouds and hung from a balcony to simulate the unfurling of sails
(E) a folded and crumpled canvas with many layers of colorful dripped and splashed paint interwoven with one another

GO ON TO THE NEXT PAGE.

3. The author mentions a collage artist in the second paragraph primarily to

(A) exemplify the style of art of the Washington Color School

(B) point out the cause of the animosity between representational artists and abstract artists

(C) establish that representational art was more popular with the general public than abstract art was

(D) illustrate the kind of art that Gilliam was reacting against

(E) show why Gilliam's art was primarily concerned with political issues

4. The passage most strongly suggests that Gilliam's attitude toward the strictly representational art of his contemporaries is which one of the following?

(A) derisive condescension

(B) open dissatisfaction

(C) whimsical dismissal

(D) careful neutrality

(E) mild approval

5. The passage says all of the following EXCEPT:

(A) Draping and folding canvases gives them a sculptural quality.

(B) Gilliam refused to satisfy the public's expectations concerning what African American art ought to address.

(C) Gilliam's views on explicitly political art were rare among African American artists.

(D) The Color Field style involved experimentation more than Gilliam believed the art of his African American contemporaries did.

(E) Everyday images such as laundry hanging out to dry are most likely to give artists great inspiration.

6. The passage suggests that Gilliam would be most likely to agree with which one of the following statements?

(A) Artists need not be concerned with aesthetic restrictions of any sort.

(B) The images portrayed in paintings, whether representational or not, should be inspired by real-life images.

(C) Artists ought to produce art that addresses the political issues of the period.

(D) The Color Field style offers artists effective ways to express the complexity of human experience.

(E) The public's expectations concerning what kind of art a certain group of artists produces should be a factor in that artist's work.

GO ON TO THE NEXT PAGE.

Passage A is from a source published in 2004 and passage B is from a source published in 2007.

Passage A

Millions of people worldwide play multiplayer online games. They each pick, say, a medieval character to play, such as a warrior. Then they might band together in quests to slay magical beasts; their

(5) avatars appear as tiny characters striding across a Tolkienesque land.

The economist Edward Castronova noticed something curious about the game he played: it had its own economy, a bustling trade in virtual goods.

(10) Players generate goods as they play, often by killing creatures for their treasure and trading it. The longer they play, the wealthier they get.

Things got even more interesting when Castronova learned about the "player auctions." Players would

(15) sometimes tire of the game and decide to sell off their virtual possessions at online auction sites.

As Castronova stared at the auction listings, he recognized with a shock what he was looking at. It was a form of currency trading! Each item had a value

(20) in the virtual currency traded in the game; when it was sold on the auction site, someone was paying cold hard cash for it. That meant that the virtual currency was worth something in real currency. Moreover, since players were killing monsters or skinning animals to

(25) sell their pelts, they were, in effect, creating wealth.

Passage B

Most multiplayer online games prohibit real-world trade in virtual items, but some actually encourage it, for example, by granting participants intellectual property rights in their creations.

(30) Although it seems intuitively the case that someone who accepts real money for the transfer of a virtual item should be taxed, what about the player who only accumulates items or virtual currency within a virtual world? Is "loot" acquired in a game taxable,

(35) as a prize or award is? And is the profit in a purely in-game trade or sale for virtual currency taxable? These are important questions, given the tax revenues at stake, and there is pressure on governments to answer them, given that the economies of some virtual

(40) worlds are comparable to those of small countries.

Most people's intuition probably would be that accumulation of assets within a game should not be taxed even though income tax applies even to noncash accessions to wealth. This article will argue that

(45) income tax law and policy support that result. Loot acquisitions in game worlds should not be treated as taxable prizes and awards, but rather should be treated like other property that requires effort to obtain, such as fish pulled from the ocean, which is taxed only

(50) upon sale. Moreover, in-game trades of virtual items should not be treated as taxable barter.

By contrast, tax doctrine and policy counsel taxation of the sale of virtual items for real currency, and, in games that are intentionally commodified,

(55) even of in-world sales for virtual currency, regardless of whether the participant cashes out. This approach would leave entertainment value untaxed without creating a tax shelter for virtual commerce.

7. Which one of the following pairs of titles would be most appropriate for passage A and passage B, respectively?

(A) "The Economic Theories of Edward Castronova"
"Intellectual Property Rights in Virtual Worlds"

(B) "An Economist Discovers New Economic Territory"
"Taxing Virtual Property"

(C) "The Surprising Growth of Multiplayer Online Games"
"Virtual Reality and the Law"

(D) "How to Make Money Playing Games"
"Closing Virtual Tax Shelters"

(E) "A New Economic Paradigm"
"An Untapped Source of Revenue"

8. Which one of the following most accurately expresses how the use of the phrase "skinning animals" in passage A (line 24) relates to the use of the phrase "fish pulled from the ocean" in passage B (line 49)?

(A) The former refers to an activity that generates wealth, whereas the latter refers to an activity that does not generate wealth.

(B) The former refers to an activity in an online game, whereas the latter refers to an analogous activity in the real world.

(C) The former, unlike the latter, refers to the production of a commodity that the author of passage B thinks should be taxed.

(D) The latter, unlike the former, refers to the production of a commodity that the author of passage B thinks should be taxed.

(E) Both are used as examples of activities by which game players generate wealth.

9. With regard to their respective attitudes toward commerce in virtual items, passage A differs from passage B in that passage A is more

(A) critical and apprehensive
(B) academic and dismissive
(C) intrigued and excited
(D) undecided but curious
(E) enthusiastic but skeptical

GO ON TO THE NEXT PAGE.

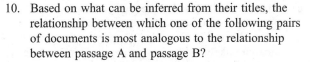

10. Based on what can be inferred from their titles, the relationship between which one of the following pairs of documents is most analogous to the relationship between passage A and passage B?

   (A)   "Advances in Artificial Intelligence"
         "Human Psychology Applied to Robots"
   (B)   "Internet Retailers Post Good Year"
         "Lawmakers Move to Tax Internet Commerce"
   (C)   "New Planet Discovered in Solar System"
         "Planet or Asteroid: Scientists Debate"
   (D)   "Biologists Create New Species in Lab"
         "Artificially Created Life: How Patent Law
         Applies"
   (E)   "A Renegade Economist's Views on Taxation"
         "Candidate Runs on Unorthodox Tax Plan"

11. The passages were most likely taken from which one of the following pairs of sources?

   (A)   passage A: a magazine article addressed to a
         general audience
         passage B: a law journal article
   (B)   passage A: a technical journal for economists
         passage B: a magazine article addressed to a
         general audience
   (C)   passage A: a science-fiction novel
         passage B: a technical journal for economists
   (D)   passage A: a law journal article
         passage B: a speech delivered before a
         legislative body
   (E)   passage A: a speech delivered before a
         legislative body
         passage B: a science-fiction novel

12. Which one of the following most accurately describes the relationship between the two passages?

   (A)   Passage A summarizes a scholar's unanticipated
         discovery, while passage B proposes solutions
         to a problem raised by the phenomenon
         discovered.
   (B)   Passage A explains an economic theory, while
         passage B identifies a practical problem
         resulting from that theory.
   (C)   Passage A reports on a subculture, while
         passage B discusses the difficulty of policing
         that subculture.
   (D)   Passage A challenges the common interpretation
         of a phenomenon, while passage B reaffirms
         that interpretation.
   (E)   Passage A states a set of facts, while passage B
         draws theoretical consequences from those facts.

13. Based on passage B, which one of the following is a characteristic of some "games that are intentionally commodified" (line 54)?

   (A)   The game allows selling real items for virtual
         currency.
   (B)   The game allows players to trade avatars with
         other players.
   (C)   Players of the game grow wealthier the longer
         they play.
   (D)   Players of the game own intellectual property
         rights in their creations.
   (E)   Players of the game can exchange one virtual
         currency for another virtual currency.

GO ON TO THE NEXT PAGE.

In certain fields of human endeavor, such as music, chess, and some athletic activities, the performance of the best practitioners is so outstanding, so superior even to the performance of other highly
(5) experienced individuals in the field, that some people believe some notion of innate talent must be invoked to account for this highest level of performance. Certain psychologists have supported this view with data concerning the performance of prodigies and the
(10) apparent heritability of relevant traits. They have noted, for example, that most outstanding musicians are discovered by the age of six, and they have found evidence that some of the qualities necessary for exceptional athletic performance, including superior
(15) motor coordination, speed of reflexes, and hand-eye coordination, can be inborn.

Until recently, however, little systematic research was done on the topic of superior performance, and previous estimates of the heritability of traits relevant
(20) to performance were based almost exclusively on random samples of the general population rather than on studies of highly trained superior performers as compared with the general population. Recent research in different domains of excellence suggests that
(25) exceptional performance arises predominantly from acquired complex skills and physiological adaptations, rather than from innate abilities. For example, it has been found that the most accomplished athletes show a systematic advantage in reaction time or perceptual
(30) discrimination only in their particular fields of performance, not in more general laboratory tests for these factors. Similarly, superior chess players have exceptional memory for configurations of chess pieces, but only if those configurations are typical of
(35) chess games.

The vast majority of exceptional adult performers were not exceptional as children, but started instruction early and improved their performance through sustained high-level training. Only extremely rarely is
(40) outstanding performance achieved without at least ten years of intensive, deliberate practice. With such intensive training, chess players who may not have superior innate capacities can acquire skills that circumvent basic limits on such factors as memory
(45) and the ability to process information. Recent research shows that, with the clear exception of some traits such as height, a surprisingly large number of anatomical characteristics, including aerobic capacity and the percentage of muscle fibers, show specific
(50) changes that develop from extended intense training.

The evidence does not, therefore, support the claim that a notion of innate talent must be invoked in order to account for the difference between good and outstanding performance, since it suggests instead that
(55) extended intense training, together with that level of talent common to all reasonably competent performers, may suffice to account for this difference. Since sustained intense training usually depends on an appropriate level of interest and desire, and since those

(60) who eventually become superior performers more often show early signs of exceptional interest than early evidence of unusual ability, motivational factors are more likely to be effective predictors of superior performance than is innate talent.

14. Which one of the following most accurately states the main point of the passage?

(A) Researchers have recently found that many inborn traits, including a surprising number of physical characteristics and motivational factors, can be altered through training and practice.

(B) Recent research into the origins of superior performance gives evidence that in sports, music, and some other fields of activity, anyone can achieve exceptional levels of performance with sustained intense practice and training.

(C) Contrary to previously accepted theories of the development of expertise, researchers have now shown that innate characteristics are irrelevant to the differences in performance among individual practitioners in various fields of activity.

(D) Recent research involving superior performers in various fields indicates that outstanding performance may result from adaptations due to training rather than from innate factors.

(E) Psychologists who previously attributed early childhood proficiency in such activities as music and chess to innate talent have revised their theories in light of new evidence of the effectiveness of training and practice.

15. Which one of the following most accurately represents the primary function of the final paragraph?

(A) It makes proposals for educational reform based on the evidence cited by the author.

(B) It demonstrates that two consequences of the findings regarding superior performance are at odds with one another.

(C) It recapitulates the evidence against the supposed heritability of outstanding talent and advocates a particular direction to be taken in future research on the topic.

(D) It raises and answers a possible objection to the author's view of the importance of intense training.

(E) It draws two inferences regarding the explanatory and predictive roles of possible factors in the development of superior performance.

GO ON TO THE NEXT PAGE.

16. Which one of the following can most reasonably be inferred from the passage?

(A) In at least some fields of human endeavor, it would be difficult, or perhaps even impossible, to ascertain whether or not a superior performer with extensive training has exceptional innate talent.

(B) Performance at the very highest level generally requires both the highest level of innate talent and many years of intensive, deliberate practice.

(C) Exceptional innate talent is a prerequisite to exceptional performance in some fields of human endeavor but not others.

(D) Exceptional innate talent is probably an obstacle to the development of superior performance, since such talent results in complacency.

(E) The importance of motivation and interest in the development of superior performance shows that in some fields the production of exceptional skill does not depend in any way on innate talents of individuals.

17. Which one of the following does the passage say is usually necessary in order for one to keep up intense practice?

(A) desire and interest
(B) emotional support from other people
(C) appropriate instruction at the right age
(D) sufficient leisure time to devote to practice
(E) self-discipline and control

18. Which one of the following most accurately describes the author's main purpose in the passage?

(A) to illustrate the ways in which a revised theoretical model can be applied to problematic cases for which previous versions of the theory offered no plausible explanation

(B) to argue that the evidence that was previously taken to support a particular theory in fact supports an opposing theory

(C) to show how a body of recent research provides evidence that certain views based on earlier research are not applicable to a particular class of cases

(D) to defend the author's new interpretation of data against probable objections that might be raised against it

(E) to explain how a set of newly formulated abstract theoretical postulations relates to a long-standing body of experimental data in a different, but related, field of inquiry

19. The passage says that superior chess players do not have exceptional memory for which one of the following?

(A) some sequences of moves that are typical of games other than chess
(B) some types of complex sequences without spatial components
(C) some chess games that have not been especially challenging
(D) some kinds of arrangements of chess pieces
(E) some types of factors requiring logical analysis in the absence of competition

GO ON TO THE NEXT PAGE.

Physicists are often asked why the image of an object, such as a chair, appears reversed left-to-right rather than, say, top-to-bottom when viewed in a mirror. Their answer is simply that an image viewed in

(5) a mirror appears reversed about the axis around which the viewer rotates his or her field of sight in turning from the object to its reflected image. That is, the reversal in question is relative to the position and orientation of the observer when the object is viewed

(10) directly. Since we ordinarily rotate our field of sight about a vertical axis, mirror images usually appear reversed left-to-right. This is the field-of-sight explanation.

However, some physicists offer a completely

(15) different explanation of what mirrors "do," suggesting that mirrors actually reverse things front-to-back. If we place a chair in front of a mirror we can envision how its reflected image will appear by imagining another chair in the space "inside" the mirror. The

(20) resulting reflection is identical to, and directly facing, the original chair. The most notable thing about this explanation is that it is clearly based on a false premise: the chair "inside" the mirror is not real, yet the explanation treats it as though it were as real and

(25) three dimensional as the original chair.

This explanation appeals strongly to many people, however, because it is quite successful at explaining what a mirror does—to a point. It seems natural because we are accustomed to dealing with our mental

(30) constructs of objects rather than with the primary sense perceptions on which those constructs are based. In general, we can safely presume a fairly reliable equation between our perceptions and their associated mental constructs, but mirrors are an exception. They

(35) present us with sense perceptions that we naturally construe in a way that is contrary to fact. Indeed, mirrors are "designed" to make a two-dimensional surface appear to have depth. Note, for example, that mirrors are among the few objects on which we

(40) almost never focus our eyes; rather, we look into them, with our focal lengths adjusted into the imagined space.

In addition to its intuitive appeal, the front-to-back explanation is motivated in part by the traditional desire in science to separate the observer

(45) from the phenomenon. Scientists like to think that what mirrors do should be explainable without reference to what the observer does (e.g., rotating a field of sight). However, questions about the appearances of images can be properly answered only

(50) if we consider both what mirrors do and what happens when we look into mirrors. If we remove the observer from consideration, we are no longer addressing images and appearances, because an image entails an observer and a point of view.

20. The main point of the passage is that an adequate explanation of mirror images

(A) must include two particular elements
(B) has yet to be determined
(C) must be determined by physicists
(D) is still subject to debate
(E) is extremely complicated

21. According to the passage, the left-to-right reversal of objects reflected in mirrors is

(A) a result of the front-to-back reversal of objects reflected in mirrors
(B) a result of the fact that we ordinarily rotate our field of sight about a vertical axis
(C) explained by the size and position of the object reflected in the mirror
(D) explained by the difference between two-dimensional and three-dimensional objects
(E) explained by the mental constructs of those who observe objects reflected in mirrors

22. According to the passage, the fact that we are accustomed to dealing with our mental constructs rather than the primary sense perceptions on which those constructs are based facilitates our ability to

(A) accept the top-to-bottom explanation of what mirrors do
(B) understand the front-to-back explanation of what mirrors do
(C) challenge complex explanations of common perceptual observations
(D) reject customarily reliable equations between perceptions and their associated mental constructs
(E) overemphasize the fact that mirrors simulate sense impressions of objects

23. It can be inferred that the author of the passage believes that the front-to-back explanation of what mirrors do is

(A) successful because it is based on incongruous facts that can be reconciled
(B) successful because it rejects any consideration of mental constructs
(C) successful because it involves the rotation of a field of sight about an axis
(D) successful only to a point because it is consistent with the traditional explanations that physicists have offered
(E) successful only to a point because it does not include what happens when we look into a mirror

GO ON TO THE NEXT PAGE.

24. In the passage the author is primarily concerned with doing which one of the following?

(A) evaluating the experimental evidence for and against two diametrically opposed explanations of a given phenomenon

(B) demonstrating that different explanations of the same phenomenon are based on different empirical observations

(C) describing the difficulties that must be overcome if a satisfactory explanation of a phenomenon is to be found

(D) showing why one explanation of a phenomenon falls short in explaining the phenomenon

(E) relating the theoretical support for an explanation of a phenomenon to the acceptance of that explanation

25. With which one of the following statements would the author of the passage be most likely to agree?

(A) The failure of one recent explanation of what mirrors do illustrates the need for better optical equipment in future experiments with mirrors.

(B) Explanations of what mirrors do generally fail because physicists overlook the differences between objects and reflections of objects.

(C) One explanation of what mirrors do reveals the traditional tendency of physicists to separate a phenomenon to be explained from the observer of the phenomenon.

(D) The degree to which human beings tend to deal directly with mental constructs rather than with primary sense perceptions depends on their training in the sciences.

(E) Considering objects reflected in mirrors to be mental constructs interferes with an accurate understanding of how primary perceptions function.

26. The author would be most likely to agree with which one of the following statements about the field-of-sight explanation of what mirrors do?

(A) This explanation is based on the traditional desire of physicists to simplify the explanation of what mirrors do.

(B) This explanation does not depend on the false premise that images in mirrors have three-dimensional properties.

(C) This explanation fails to take into account the point of view and orientation of someone who is observing reflections in the mirror.

(D) This explanation assumes that people who see something in a mirror do not understand the reality of what they see.

(E) This explanation is unsuccessful because it involves claims about how people rotate their field of sight rather than claims about what people can imagine.

27. The author mentions the fact that we rarely focus our eyes on mirrors (lines 39–40) primarily in order to

(A) contrast our capacity to perceive objects with our capacity to imagine objects

(B) emphasize that it is impossible to perceive reflected objects without using mental constructs of the objects

(C) clarify the idea that mirrors simulate three-dimensional reality

(D) illustrate the fact that we typically deal directly with mental constructs rather than with perceptions

(E) emphasize the degree to which the psychological activity of the observer modifies the shape of the object being perceived

S T O P

IF YOU FINISH BEFORE TIME IS CALLED, YOU MAY CHECK YOUR WORK ON THIS SECTION ONLY. DO NOT WORK ON ANY OTHER SECTION IN THE TEST.

Acknowledgment is made to the following sources from which material has been adapted for use in this test booklet:

"A Mirror to Physics." ©1997 by Kevin Brown.

Gerard Audesirk and Teresa Audesirk, *Biology*, 3rd ed. ©1993 by Macmillan Publishing Company.

K. Anders Ericsson and Neil Charness, "Expert Performance: Its Structure and Acquisition." ©1994 by the American Psychological Association, Inc.

Leandra Lederman, "'Stranger than Fiction': Taxing Virtual Worlds." ©2007 by New York University Law Review.

Regenia A. Perry, *Free within Ourselves*. ©1992 by the Smithsonian Institution.

Clive Thompson, "Game Theories." ©2004 by The Walrus Magazine.

Wait for the supervisor's instructions before you open the page to the topic.
Please print and sign your name and write the date in the designated spaces below.

Time: 35 Minutes

General Directions

will have 35 minutes in which to plan and write an essay on the topic inside. Read the topic and the accompanying directions carefully. will probably find it best to spend a few minutes considering the topic and organizing your thoughts before you begin writing. In your essay, sure to develop your ideas fully, leaving time, if possible, to review what you have written. **Do not write on a topic other than the one cified. Writing on a topic of your own choice is not acceptable.**

special knowledge is required or expected for this writing exercise. Law schools are interested in the reasoning, clarity, organization, juage usage, and writing mechanics displayed in your essay. How well you write is more important than how much you write.

fine your essay to the blocked, lined area on the front and back of the separate Writing Sample Response Sheet. Only that area will be roduced for law schools. Be sure that your writing is legible.

Both this topic sheet and your response sheet must be turned in to the testing staff
before you leave the room.

Topic Code
118340

Print Your Full Name Here		
Last	First	M.I.

Date
/   /

Sign Your Name Here

Scratch Paper
Do not write your essay in this space.

LSAT® Writing Sample Topic

Directions: The scenario presented below describes two choices, either one of which can be supported on the basis of the information given. Your essay should consider both choices and argue for one over the other, based on the two specified criteria and the facts provided. There is no "right" or "wrong" choice: a reasonable argument can be made for either.

An organization whose members are professors in a certain discipline holds an important annual conference centered around a full schedule of academic presentations. Most job interviews for positions in the discipline are also conducted at this conference. The organization is deciding whether to continue holding the conference on its usual meeting dates or to hold it two weeks later. Using the facts below, write an essay in which you argue for one option over the other based on the following two criteria:

- The organization wants to encourage its members to attend the conference.
- The organization wants to encourage attendees to go to conference presentations.

The usual meeting dates fall at a time when none of the members' universities hold classes, just after a major family-oriented holiday. In order to spend more time with their families, many potential conference attendees do not attend. The organization recently began offering lodging subsidies and childcare to make attending with family more attractive. Some conference attendees now spend time with their families that they could spend attending presentations. Many members attend the conference to conduct interviews, which take up most of their time. Air travel to the conference is very expensive during the usual meeting dates. Hotel accommodations cost less than at any other time of year.

The later dates fall at a time when a relatively small percentage of members' universities hold classes. These members would be unable to attend or conduct interviews at the conference. No holidays occur within a week of the later dates. The organization could take the money it currently spends on lodging subsidies and childcare and use it to fund additional presentations of interest to more of its members. Air travel is much less expensive during the later dates. Hotel accommodations cost somewhat more.

WP-U11

Scratch Paper
Do not write your essay in this space.

COMPUTING YOUR SCORE

Directions:

1. Use the Answer Key on the next page to check your answers.

2. Use the Scoring Worksheet below to compute your raw score.

3. Use the Score Conversion Chart to convert your raw score into the 120–180 scale.

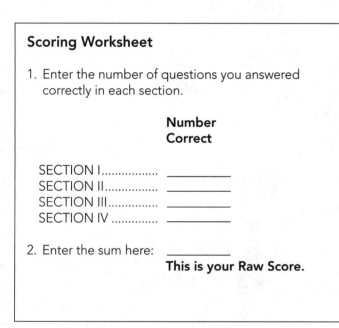

Scoring Worksheet

1. Enter the number of questions you answered correctly in each section.

	Number Correct
SECTION I.................	_____
SECTION II................	_____
SECTION III..............	_____
SECTION IV	_____

2. Enter the sum here: _____
   This is your Raw Score.

Conversion Chart
For Converting Raw Score to the 120–180 LSAT Scaled Score
LSAT Form 3LSN104

Reported Score	Raw Score Lowest	Raw Score Highest
180	98	101
179	97	97
178	96	96
177	95	95
176	94	94
175	93	93
174	92	92
173	90	91
172	89	89
171	88	88
170	87	87
169	85	86
168	84	84
167	82	83
166	81	81
165	79	80
164	78	78
163	76	77
162	75	75
161	73	74
160	72	72
159	70	71
158	68	69
157	67	67
156	65	66
155	63	64
154	62	62
153	60	61
152	58	59
151	57	57
150	55	56
149	54	54
148	52	53
147	51	51
146	49	50
145	47	48
144	46	46
143	44	45
142	43	43
141	41	42
140	40	40
139	38	39
138	37	37
137	35	36
136	34	34
135	33	33
134	31	32
133	30	30
132	29	29
131	28	28
130	27	27
129	25	26
128	24	24
127	23	23
126	22	22
125	21	21
124	20	20
123	19	19
122	18	18
121	17	17
120	0	16

ANSWER KEY

SECTION I

1.	E	8.	D	15.	B	22.	E
2.	D	9.	A	16.	B	23.	C
3.	D	10.	C	17.	B	24.	E
4.	D	11.	E	18.	C	25.	D
5.	E	12.	B	19.	A		
6.	D	13.	A	20.	C		
7.	E	14.	C	21.	C		

SECTION II

1.	E	8.	C	15.	B	22.	E
2.	A	9.	B	16.	D	23.	B
3.	E	10.	C	17.	C		
4.	D	11.	E	18.	A		
5.	A	12.	A	19.	C		
6.	A	13.	A	20.	E		
7.	B	14.	C	21.	A		

SECTION III

1.	C	8.	C	15.	A	22.	B
2.	D	9.	D	16.	B	23.	E
3.	B	10.	A	17.	C	24.	A
4.	E	11.	A	18.	D	25.	A
5.	C	12.	A	19.	D	26.	E
6.	D	13.	E	20.	B		
7.	A	14.	B	21.	A		

SECTION IV

1.	A	8.	B	15.	E	22.	B
2.	E	9.	C	16.	A	23.	E
3.	D	10.	D	17.	A	24.	D
4.	B	11.	A	18.	C	25.	C
5.	E	12.	A	19.	D	26.	B
6.	D	13.	D	20.	A	27.	C
7.	B	14.	D	21.	B		